T0118443

James Van Norwood Ellis, MD

TRIUMPHS, TRAGEDIES, AND TEARS:

Life Journey of a Mid-South Doctor, Part One

iUniverse, Inc.
Bloomington

Triumphs, Tragedies, and Tears:
Life Journey of a Mid-South Doctor, Part One

iUniverse books may be ordered through booksellers or by contacting:

iUniverse
1663 Liberty Drive
Bloomington, IN 47403
www.iuniverse.com
1-800-Authors (1-800-288-4677)

Because of the dynamic nature of the Internet, any web addresses or links contained in this book may have changed since publication and may no longer be valid. The views expressed in this work are solely those of the author and do not necessarily reflect the views of the publisher, and the publisher hereby disclaims any responsibility for them.

Any people depicted in stock imagery provided by Thinkstock are models, and such images are being used for illustrative purposes only.

Certain stock imagery © Thinkstock.

ISBN: 978-1-4620-3382-9 (sc)
ISBN: 978-1-4620-3383-6 (e)
ISBN: 978-1-4620-3809-1 (dj)

Printed in the United States of America

iUniverse rev. date: 9/1/2011

Dedication

This book is dedicated to the love of my life, my wife Brenda, and to the millions out there with Multiple Sclerosis.

CONTENTS

Preface

I have been encouraged to write my story, the story of my life's journey, by many individuals. It took a cataclysmic life event—my suicide attempt—to compel me to finally write my story. I felt it was important to share the events in my life that helped shape me into the individual I have become. I hope that my story will be beneficial to others who have experienced or will experience similar life events. I pray that the contents of this book inspire and give hope for a national dialogue to address the issues of suicide, mental illness, and continued racism, especially in the medical profession. I pray for second chances for those of us who have made mistakes in life. God gave me a second chance; shouldn't we as human beings do the same for our fellow man?

I would like to thank my family, Brenda, Courtney, and Van, for their unwavering support. I have never felt closer to Brenda or loved her more than now. I am blessed and thankful for the friendship and support of attorney William Heaton. I would like to thank the many individuals who sent letters and cards of support during my hospitalization and incarceration.

Introduction

This book represents part one of my life's journey. Part two will be forthcoming in the near future. The events in this book are true. Actual names of individuals and institutions were changed to protect privacy and anonymity.

CHAPTER 1

Early Years

How did I get here? What happened? I was a successful physician, well-respected by everyone. Well, maybe not everyone, but certainly by most. I had traveled far along life's journey, from a little boy on welfare without a father, to being a devoted father and, yes, a devoted husband. I had been blessed with a wonderful wife, daughter, and son. I tried to please everyone, tried to make everyone happy. I did everything for everyone! I freely gave of myself, my time, my money, and my heart, to my family and to my patients. Yet, here I sit in a dark cell, completely naked, with nothing to lie on except cold concrete and steel. Despite all of the good I had done with my life, here I am in jail on suicide watch. I fucked up! I gave up on life, tried to commit suicide, and committed a serious crime during the attempt—a crime I don't remember. What I did was wrong, and this is the punishment I deserve. I close my eyes and cry. For some unexplained reason, the course of my entire life began to play like a movie in my mind, starting from the beginning.

James Van Norwood Ellis, what a mouthful! I was the firstborn child of James and Catherine Sims Ellis. I arrived on the eleventh of February 1951, one of millions of baby boomers born to the World War II generation. My sister, Ina, was born one year later. We all moved to Richmond, Virginia, just after my second birthday. The move was necessary in order for my dad to keep his job when the company he worked for relocated. That said, my dad was born and grew up in Richmond, so he was returning home. My first memory of Richmond is from my early childhood. I was lying on my abdomen on the plush lawn of my backyard. As in a fairy tale, the setting is always absolutely serene. I felt that God was displaying his handiwork especially for me. I lay there in the grass, not thinking, but absorbing nature's display in my own backyard. Butterflies of all varieties floated by while flocks of birds flew overhead, calling to each other in a language only they understood. A myriad of insects including bumblebees and hornets methodically sampled dandelions and other wildflowers in my backyard. It was an early spring day with dew still glistening on blades of grass, the sun framed by a cloudless and seemingly endless blue sky. *Yes*, I thought to myself, *life is good*. I felt special, chosen; I definitely felt that I was the golden child. I was smart, energetic, and happy.

Mom, Dad, and just about everyone addressed me by my middle name, Van. Dad was reserved: quiet, but feared. His stout frame with large arms and legs projected a powerful image. There was no doubt that he was an athlete, and indeed he had been. He was an all-state running back in high school and was very popular and well-liked. He was to attend Virginia Union University on a full football scholarship, but World War II interrupted his plans to attend college. America declared war on Japan and its allies, Germany and Italy, following the Japanese surprise attack on Pearl Harbor, during which more than two thousand American servicemen died. A massive sentiment of rage and disgust against the Japanese swept the country; everyone wanted revenge. Dad volunteered shortly after his eighteenth birthday in December of 1941. He was assigned to the Third Army, under General George S. Patton. Dad never talked about the war except occasionally when I inquired about his military service. When I was a small boy, I remembered sitting with him on the couch watching the Gillette Friday Night Fights. He enjoyed watching boxing and would tell me about his military service and how he boxed for the army during the war. Many years later, I discovered how patriotic he was. He was angrier at the Nazis than at the Japanese because of their racism; he remembered how Joe Louis and Jesse Owens were received in Germany. The reports of Nazi concentration camps and the mass murder of Jews enraged him. Many years later, I discovered information from old family records that he was possibly part Jewish on his father's side.

Mom was tall, with flawless ebony skin. She grew up in Meridian, Mississippi, the youngest of eleven children. I never met her father but do remember one visit from her mother, who had the same flawless skin with long, silky black hair down to her waist. She was part Choctaw Indian. Mom ran the house, doing the cooking, cleaning, washing, and ironing. There were not enough hours in the day to keep up with all the work, but Mom always smiled. As the eldest, I helped as much as I could with the chores. By my fifth birthday, our family had five kids—a baby born every year. You can imagine that it was hectic, but my mother never took shortcuts. She made all meals with fresh ingredients every day, and on Sunday, meals were exceptional. My absolute favorite meal was golden-brown fried chicken, mashed potatoes, gravy, greens (collards, turnips, or both), and mouth-watering homemade rolls that melted in your mouth. Occasionally she served roast beef or turkey instead of chicken. Dessert always included homemade ice cream, which I enjoyed helping to make.

Mom was the front-line disciplinarian, and quite good at it! She had a talent for always picking one of those stinging green switches. When Mom was not enough, Dad would take over discipline. Therefore, I tried hard to stay on my parents' good sides.

I started elementary school at age five. The morning of

my first day of school, I was up early. I got dressed and ate breakfast. While waiting to walk to school, I made a toy to play with to pass the time. I made most of my toys. On this morning, I made a toy from a string and metallic nut. I twirled my new toy in a wide circle as fast as I could. Then, without warning, the whirling metallic nut crashed into my left eyebrow, leaving a nasty gash. Thank goodness it missed my eye! Mom bandaged my cut, and then I was off to school.

I was very eager to start school. It was the forum that I needed to get the attention I craved at home. I became the teacher's pet quickly; I seemed to know all the answers, which made me the center of attention. I enjoyed being in the limelight. The school curriculum seemed so easy that by second grade, I had developed the attitude that I did not need to complete assigned homework because I was so smart. My second-grade teacher brought me back to reality with a dose of corporal punishment. I never failed to complete any homework after that.

I became well-known to all the teachers at my elementary school by third grade as "Mr. Straight As." My mom, however, was not impressed by my school grades. She thought it was a waste for a black man to get an education. She would say, "What good is an education when it doesn't help you get a decent job? What kind of work can you do besides a desk job? If you want to earn a decent wage and support a family, you need to get a good-paying factory job." I was hurt deeply by her comments and vowed to prove her wrong. I believed that getting an education was best for my future success. I realized what an education had done for many of the teachers who were my mentors. My dad appeared to be neutral about the value of an education. However, one of my Christmas presents from him, which I still treasure, was a chalk board and white chalk. He called me, "The Little Professor."

Mom and Dad began to have marital problems by my seventh birthday. It appeared to be related to Mom's recent embrace of the Seventh Day Adventist Church. My dad rebelled because he would have to give up smoking cigarettes, drinking beer, and eating pork. Surprisingly, he became a church member and behaved for one year, after which their relationship began to deteriorate rapidly. Dad became bitter about the dietary restrictions. He hated not smoking, and occasionally I would catch him sneaking a smoke. It seemed to me that the straw that broke the camel's back was the matter of paying tithes. I overheard many bitter arguments between my parents regarding tithing. Dad would argue that he did not understand why he had to pay ten percent of his hard-earned income that was desperately needed to provide for our growing family, which included six kids. His refusal to pay tithes caused mom to retaliate by leaving with all six of us kids in tow. By my eighth birthday, they had reconciled with Dad agreeing to tithe. However, the truce was short-lived. The fighting and arguing started again in less than six months. Physical abuse restarted, and escalated quickly. I was brave enough to try to stop my dad, but my eight-year-old self presented no physical threat. He easily tossed me aside, like the wind blowing a leaf.

Mom and Dad separated again, and shortly thereafter, Dad disappeared, leaving my mother with six hungry kids to feed without financial support. We quickly found ourselves homeless, living with church members until mom could obtain public assistance and public housing. I began to hate my life. I hated the old or ragged clothes, holes in my shoes, and constant hunger. My best meal was lunch at school. My welfare ticket usually granted me a hot meal including dessert and milk. Meals at home had generally gone meatless, consisting of white beans and cornbread; breakfast was either cream of wheat or oatmeal. Food serving sizes at home were always meager, so getting big portions free at school was a real treat.

As time passed, my hunger overtook my pride. I would quickly eat my entire lunch, take my empty tray back to the tray return area, and then wait for others turning in trays with food still on them that I would devour. Several of my peers conspired to mock me; they started dumping their leftover food into the trash right in front of me, saying, "Oh James, I'm so sorry! I forgot that you are poor and hungry." Once they walked away, I quickly grabbed anything edible dumped in the trash and gobbled it. Soon, I lost any pride I had left, grabbing leftovers before they hit the garbage can. I became the subject of many cruel jokes. However, I didn't care; I was hungry and had found a way to get the additional nutrition I needed. Some of the teachers began to pay attention to my actions and ordered me away from the tray return area. One day, a teacher was stationed at the food tray return area, putting an end to my food bonanza. I cried, not loudly but in a dignified manner, with no noise, just tears streaming down my face.

As I suffered quietly, a teacher approached me, gently placed her hand on my shoulder, and spoke to me softly as a mother would speak to her own son. "Young man, don't cry" she said, drying my tears with a soft white tissue. "Please come to my classroom with me. I have something for you."

"Yes, ma'am," I replied. Her classroom was located just down the hall leading from the cafeteria. I saw her name on the door: Mrs. Lillian Epps, Fifth Grade. My spirits lifted! I had heard about Mrs. Epps. Everyone wanted to be in her class. She was regarded as one of the best teachers by all students and teachers. It went beyond being lucky if you were in her class; you were blessed. She turned to speak to me after we entered her classroom. "James, I am so sorry about your home situation. I know you must be very hungry. Here, take this sandwich and apple. I want you to eat it. Go ahead, sit down."

Eagerly, I took the food. The sandwich was pimento cheese. *Yummy!* I thought as I chewed happily.

Smiling, Mrs. Epps asked, "How is it?"

"Wonderful!" I replied. "Thank you so much, Mrs. Epps!"

"You are most welcome, dear." Her face grew serious. "Now, James, I don't want to see you eating off of the food trays and out of the garbage can. I will look for you every day and make sure you have had enough to eat. Okay?"

"Yes, ma'am," I said and nodded.

She continued, "You are a very good student with a bright future. I want you in my class. I want to encourage you to continue to study hard and do well. Your future is very bright if you continue performing well and doing your best."

"I would love to be in your class. Thank you so much!"

"You are welcome!" she replied with her soft hand touching my face. "How does your stomach feel now?"

"Wonderful!" I floated out of her classroom and quickly proceeded to my own fourth-grade room still wearing a broad smile as I took my seat. That day I started to believe in angels. Surely Mrs. Epps was one.

Fourth grade ended uneventfully. Summer bought an unexpected surprise. The stress of being a single mom with an army of hungry kids took its toll on my mother. There was never enough money or food, but Mom still gave tithes to the church, which added further economic stress, and the cavalry to help or rescue us was nowhere in sight. Many nights I listened to Mom cry and pray. One morning she refused to get up. I did the best I could helping my brothers and sisters prepare for school, but each morning that Mom stayed in bed it got more difficult. Neighbors and teachers began to notice that we looked dirtier, shabbier, and hungrier. One day I arrived home and Mom was gone. I panicked. One of my neighbors informed me that several people from the state had taken her away. I found out later that she had been confined to a mental hospital because she had suffered a nervous breakdown.

The first night my brothers, sisters, and I were alone, my fear and panic evolved into a resolute determination to carry on, to survive, and to care for my siblings. The next morning, I decided to make money. It was common practice for boys my age to gather outside of the front of a grocery store and offer to help individuals with their groceries. Since most patrons walked to the grocery store, I offered to carry their groceries in my red wagon (my Christmas present from my dad prior to his disappearance). I charged a quarter for this service; the first day I earned $1.50. I used the money to buy bread, our food for the day. A whole week passed, and every afternoon I returned home with whatever I could afford to buy—usually just bread. One morning, just before I was about to leave the house, a black car with a large emblem on its door stopped in front of the house we were renting. I could see the words *State of Virginia* on the car door, and I knew instantly that it must be welfare people. All six of us crowded into the car and were delivered to foster homes. My sister Ina and I were fortunate enough to go to Uncle Harry and Aunt Maria. The rest of my siblings were placed in strangers' homes.

Uncle Harry was my father's eldest brother. He and his wife had two children, my cousins Cookie and Joe. My sister Janice was placed with relatives of Aunt Maria who lived next door. Both Cookie and Joe were older than I, four years and ten years respectively. We all seemed to tolerate each other well. Cookie had just started high school; Joe had recently joined the United States Marine Corps. They weren't really academic, so I was considered rather odd because I loved to read, especially books about science and scientists.

I cleaned up cousin Joe's old bike and began exploring Richmond, thrilled to have transportation to the state and city libraries to read more books about science and invention. My heroes were George Washington Carver and Thomas Edison, particularly the latter, because he and I shared the same birthday. In those days, science was on everyone's mind. The Russians' recent launch of the first satellite to orbit the Earth stunned the United States, which, until this event, had felt that it was the world leader in scientific advancement. The launch of Sputnik was a reality check for the United States. The USSR sent a message to the world that they had become the leader in science, math, and discovery. President Kennedy issued a challenge to all Americans—especially the youth—to meet and surpass the apparent Soviet technological edge. He challenged America to place a man on the moon by the end of the decade. I accepted this challenge; I would become a scientist.

I entered fifth grade energized by my goal. I also eagerly anticipated being assigned to Mrs. Epps' class. She assigned me to a seat in the front row, the typical location for the teacher's pet. Aware of my passion for science, she always called on me to answer when no one volunteered. With a smile, she'd say, "I bet James knows the answer!" Usually I did, because of my extensive summer reading—all those science and mathematics books!

I didn't realize it until later, but Mrs. Epps was one of those special human beings dedicated to the teaching profession. She was my first mentor. She wanted me to become knowledgeable in all subjects, including music, the arts, and etiquette. She really encouraged me to develop and pursue my creative side. I discovered I was quite a good artist. She encouraged me to play a musical instrument, presenting me with a flute for which I was most grateful. I immediately joined the school band, learned how to play the flute, and played with the group for the rest of elementary school. I also designed and produced most of the background scenery for all our plays, several of which I wrote. I also wrote poems and short stories. To round out my education, Mrs. Epps invited me to her home for dinner on several occasions. Not only were the meals wonderful, but we also practiced table manners. I thought to myself, *This is how I want to live*. I wanted to be cultured, creative, knowledgable in all things: the essence of a Renaissance man. Mrs. Epps inspired me to dream and believe that my dreams could become true.

I kept in touch with Mrs. Epps throughout my life; I wanted to inform her of my progress. She was always supportive of me and proud of my achievements. I thank God for her mentoring.

Mrs. Epps inspired me to dream and believe that my dreams could become true.

She was truly an angel—the first of several who appeared at crucial periods in my life.

I was sad when it was time to graduate from fifth grade and leave Mrs. Epps' nurturing environment. My sixth-grade teacher was no Mrs. Epps, but she, like many African American teachers of that era, was totally dedicated to nurturing, educating, and encouraging young black minds. This was their duty, their mission, and their contribution to the greater good of American society. I, like many others of my generation, was a product of this dedication.

1962. The Cold War between the United States and the Soviet Union dominated the news. The recent failure of the United States-sponsored Bay of Pigs military operation in Cuba had escalated tensions. The Soviets had responded by placing missiles in communist Cuba, some probably nuclear. I and my peers, as well as adults, were all petrified that World War III was imminent. We knew that a nuclear war would end human civilization as we knew it. Kennedy's bold decision to establish a naval blockade of Cuba to prevent the delivery of nuclear warheads had the potential to backfire and ignite a nuclear conflict. As the time approached for the Soviet ships to be stopped and boarded, all prayed that it would not be the last sunset mankind would witness. I remembered not sleeping well that night. I dreamed of mushroom clouds appearing on the horizon.

I awoke to the soft rays of the dawn sun streaming through the window of my bedroom. I was still alive! The naval blockade had worked! The morning news confirmed its success: Soviet ships had been turned back, and the missiles were being removed from Cuba. Khrushchev, the Soviet leader, regarded as a bully by many, had been defeated, and President Kennedy was a hero!

For the first time in my life I had begun to realize that society was divided along racial lines. More importantly, I began to realize the implications of being African American in America: my dreams were limited. Maybe Mom was right after all. President Kennedy's election raised the expectations of African Americans, who had dreamed for a president like Kennedy. Centuries of enslavement, frustration, and limitations on our freedoms of life, liberty, and the pursuit of happiness all welled up behind the wall of imposed second-class citizenship. To long-suffering blacks, the Kennedy administration breached this wall. The momentum for change had grown into a strong national civil rights movement, led by Dr. Martin Luther King Jr. I witnessed the March on Washington in 1963, sensing that history was being made before my very eyes. Dr. King's resounding voice and clear eloquence spoke to my heart; his words, "Let freedom ring," will forever resonate in my consciousness and in that of all Americans. There was no turning back for America.

I entered seventh grade with renewed enthusiasm for the future. This was junior high school, and the beginning of separate classrooms and teachers for each subject. My classes and teachers were all excellent, but I was partial to my science teacher, Mr. Lawrence, who was also my band instructor. He taught chemistry as well, a subject I thoroughly enjoyed. His encouragement helped me decide to major in chemistry later in college, while his patient instruction led me to a mastery of the flute. Mr. Lawrence was my first important male mentor.

In late fall, thoughts of the approaching holiday season were on my mind. November 23, 1963, seemed like any other fall day: cool crisp air, the fading fall foliage, bright but shortening daylight. It was midday; my history class was almost over and our stomachs reminded us it was nearly lunchtime. Suddenly, a frantic knock on the classroom door interrupted my concentration. My history teacher was summoned from the classroom; she returned shortly, sobbing profusely. She was barely able to utter the devastating news, "President Kennedy is dead! He was shot. We may have another Civil War!" *Oh my God,* I thought. This could mean the end of the many hopes and dreams of Americans, especially African Americans. My teacher continued to sob uncontrollably while I and the other students sat mute, stunned. The silence was broken by an announcement that the school day had ended out of respect for the president.

I walked home slowly, desperately trying to make sense of it all. Why would someone want to kill the president? He had tried to help everyone! He had such promise. Now the dreams of a people and a nation would be lost. I arrived home before my sister Ina. We did not talk, but our silence spoke volumes. Uncle Harry, Aunt Maria, and Cookie got home less than thirty minutes later. We were all glued to the special news coverage of the assassination on television when we heard a loud knock at the front door. Aunt Maria invited in a medium-sized white lady dressed in dark clothes. Ina and I were called to meet the stranger, a representative of the state welfare agency. She informed us that our mom had been released from the mental institution, and was cleared to get custody of her children. Quietly, Aunt Maria said, "Van, Ina get your things. Your mom wants you all back."

I had not fully recovered from the shocking Kennedy assassination news; this was another jolt that made my head spin. I had mixed emotions. Mom was well again—that was good news. The bad news was that I would be transferred to another school, have to go back on welfare, and return to the days of tattered clothing and constant hunger. My sisters and I sat in silence as we rode to be reunited with mom. We were unusually solemn, highly contrary to our generally playful demeanor. I stared out of the window at passing cars as the surroundings morphed from familiar to unfamiliar. I began to feel engulfed by helplessness and hopelessness. We had lost our president and our comfortable home all in one day.

An hour passed before we arrived at the apartment building where we would be reunited with our mother. My other brothers and sisters had already arrived. It had been more than three years since I had seen Victor, Linda, Michael, and David. Victor was eight, Linda seven, Michael six, and David just four years old. I was the oldest at twelve; Ina was eleven; Janice would be ten the next month. Additionally, Mom informed us that we had a baby sister, Iris, born in 1960, and a baby brother named Julius who had just turned one; the little ones were still in foster homes. Nine of us! I looked at my brothers' and sisters' sad eyes, seeing and feeling the pain and abuse they had all endured. I started to cry and reached to embrace all of them. Mom joined us, and she too began to cry. Mom kissed all of us and told each of us how much she had missed all of her babies. She sighed, "Thank God, children, we are a family again! Now let us pray." We all got on our knees and recited the Lord's prayer as she had taught us long ago.

Mom showed us to our bedrooms, all boys in one and the girls in another. Mom slept in the third bedroom. She had already prepared dinner, which was of course meatless: white beans, slaw, and corn bread. There was no doubt that we would return to the Seventh-day Adventist church. I had a flashback to all the "forbidden" foods that I had enjoyed while at Uncle Harry's—specifically pork, which I loved, particularly when barbecued. Now we would go to church on Saturday instead of Sunday and I would miss going to the movie theater afterward, as was customary at Uncle Harry's. Yes, life with Mom would be more restrictive—certainly not a bad thing, but would take some time for me to adjust to our new routine.

Within two weeks we moved across town to a larger apartment in a government housing complex. My siblings and I enrolled in the neighborhood school to finish the school year. I hated our new situation. The housing complex was in a tough neighborhood. Most of the families were like ours: absent father, lots of kids, surviving on welfare. Many of the children didn't bother going to school, loitering around the complex, and thanks to the inevitable boredom and unhappiness, fights broke out nearly every day. Usually the girls were safe, but the boys had to fight to prove that they belonged.

Then there were the gangs. The gang that controlled our neighborhood tried to recruit my brother Victor and me. I informed the pair who stopped us that we weren't interested. These were fighting words; immediately they assumed an attack stance. Victor was only eight but had thick, muscular arms and legs, like our dad, whereas I was a scrawny twelve-year-old, no match for the two gang members. Suddenly, one of them knocked me to the ground. Before I could gather my senses and stand up, Victor had knocked both of them to the ground. They scrambled up and disappeared.

Victor helped me to my feet and asked, "Van, are you okay? I wasn't going to let them beat you up!"

"Wow," I replied. "Yeah, Victor, I'm all right! Where did you learn to fight like that?" Victor shrugged. "I don't know. I am pretty strong, I guess."

Damn, I thought, *just like dad*! We walked back to the apartment, tacitly in agreement that we wouldn't tell Mom any of what transpired.

The next day Victor and I were walking home from the store with groceries when another two thugs confronted us. We both knew we had to fight, so we put the grocery bags down. Before anyone uttered a word, Victor hit both of the toughs, knocking them to the ground. They got up and ran as fast as they could in the opposite direction. Victor and I laughed, picked up the groceries, and went home. After that, we didn't have any more trouble from gangs—or anyone else for that matter.

My classes at the new school in our neighborhood were not at all challenging. I was quickly moved to a class for advanced students, where I continued to perform well, especially with science and math courses; I usually finished my science and math homework during homeroom before the end of the school day. I had a few friends at school who wanted my help with homework, but they ignored me after school. I didn't mind that; as poor as we all were, I looked forward to going home every day to be with my family.

Fall 1964 appeared on time; nature's foliage display was just starting. We moved again, to a newer government housing apartment with four bedrooms. Julius, my baby brother, finally joined us, although Iris remained with her foster family she started with. I later learned that Mom moved often to avoid my dad. Apparently he would track Mom down, show up unexpectedly, impregnate her (that was how Iris and Julius were conceived), and then disappear. By this time, I had developed negative feelings about my home situation. I felt like Dad hated us. Why was he treating us this way? I did not like the way Mom seemed to protect him or how often she got pregnant by him. I resented both of them for our welfare lives. I promised myself that when I grew up, I would never treat my family that way.

Our new neighborhood was also adjacent to a brand-new junior and senior high school. I was assigned to an advanced eighth-grade class of approximately fifteen students. The curriculum consisted of senior-high courses. It was refreshing for me to be among students considered to be some of the best in Richmond public schools. We studied together and supported each other; all of us wanted the entire group to perform well. Moreover, our guidance counselor seemed to give all of us specialized attention. Every two weeks she tested the group using standardized exams. We weren't sure exactly why, but we didn't mind the rigor of the program.

In the spring, our guidance counselor informed about ten of us that we had consistently performed well on testing and would be given an aptitude test for special admissions to private preparatory schools in New England. If we performed well, all expenses for four years would be paid for from a special scholarship fund. Amazingly, every one of us qualified! We were ecstatic! Very prestigious private preparatory schools in New England had granted us acceptance; the group would be attending such institutions as Deerfield, Northfield Mount Hermon, Choate Hall, Philips Exeter, and Cushing Academy.

My classmates and I hugged each other in celebration. Suddenly, though, a sobering thought occurred to me: my mom might not give her consent for me to pursue this opportunity. I thought that maybe I could persuade her to let me go if I explained to her how important this opportunity was for me. I could not wait to get home that evening to try to convince her. As I'd expected, however, she immediately refused to let me accept the scholarship opportunity. I was crushed; I even thought about running away from home. Instead, I dragged myself to school the next day and reported that I had to turn down the scholarship because my mom wouldn't let me go. It was one of the hardest things I have ever done. The guidance counselor tried to persuade my mom to reconsider, but that was unsuccessful. My dreams for my future started to fizzle away.

Mom's behavior began to deteriorate rapidly near the end of the school year; I suspected that she was not taking her medication. Her lack of ability to cope with the stress of raising seven hungry children rendered her irrational, temperamental, and out of touch with reality. Money and food usually ran out two weeks into each month. Relief in the form of gifted food from church and neighbors helped, but still my siblings and I cried ourselves to sleep most nights because of hunger. Mom's mental state became so dire that neighbors began talking about our situation, and I am sure some of them called authorities to report our situation. Eventually, Mom began to hear voices and hallucinate. I knew that soon she would be hospitalized again. Predictably, Mom wound up in another mental facility. Again, like several years earlier, we children found ourselves alone for several days. As the school year ended, my siblings and I stared into a dark, uncertain future.

Then, a miracle happened. Our fraternal grandfather and his young wife Dorothy, from Chattanooga, Tennessee, happened to be visiting relatives in Richmond. We never saw them much except on special occasions like holidays. It was the last week of June; the July Fourth holiday was one week away. Granddaddy and Dorothy (whom we called "Big Mama") paid us a surprise visit! Most of my siblings did not know or remember Granddad, but I did. I was given his middle name Norwood. There were family rumors that Mom, Dad, Granddad, and Big Mama were all married on the same day in Chattanooga. Big Mama was a full-figured young woman with smooth ebony skin, but the really stunning thing about her was that she was three years younger than my dad! Granddaddy married her when she was twenty-four and he was fifty-five. We all loved her; she had an infectious smile. My granddad's eyes always seemed to sparkle in her presence. She was an extraordinary cook; I remembered my parents telling me how I use to crawl behind Big Momma as an infant, crying to get a taste of her biscuits and gravy, the only food I wanted to eat instead of baby food.

Whenever Granddaddy and Big Mama came to Richmond, they stayed at my aunt Evelyn's house, which became the gathering place for family members in town. Granddaddy had just retired and was thinking of moving back to Richmond. However, Big Mama wanted to stay in Chattanooga near her family. She desperately wanted children but had never gotten pregnant. My brothers, sisters, and I were just about to be distributed to foster homes, but, realizing a perfect solution, Big Mama interceded on our behalf and pleaded with Granddaddy to take all of us back to Chattanooga. We would be an instant family for her—she wanted all eight of us! She would have taken all nine, in fact, but little Iris had been adopted by her foster parents. The welfare agency was more than happy to release all of us into their custody. We all would be a family. Big Mama and Granddaddy came to give us the good news: we were all going to Chattanooga in the morning!

At the break of dawn, all of us crowded into two vehicles and headed to the train station to depart for Chattanooga. We left with only the clothes on our backs. I don't remember many details of the train ride; we were all tired, but we were happy to be together. We must have slept nearly the entire ride. I do remember awakening to the early streaks of light cast by the rising sun barely visible as the train navigated the final mountains and hills surrounding the approach to Chattanooga. It was dawn on Independence Day. Big Mama had called her family prior to leaving Richmond. We were told that there would be a huge family gathering to celebrate the holiday. It would also be an opportunity to meet members of her family and relatives.

It took about thirty minutes to reach the cozy white-frame home sitting atop a small hill. Well-manicured waist-high green shrubs served as a front yard border. The driveway was long enough to accommodate four cars. The backyard contained a small garden, separated from the rest of the yard by wire fencing. Inside we found three bedrooms, a living room, a kitchen/dining room area, and two bathrooms. While large enough for Big Mama and Granddaddy, it would be a tight fit for an additional eight kids. Still, Big Mama appeared energized. Granddaddy sat in his recliner, lit up one of his favorite cigars and watched his young wife take charge. Big Mama and those of us who were large enough moved suitcases into the master bedroom. She then told the girls to follow her to the kitchen to help prepare breakfast. The boys sat at Granddaddy's feet as he began to talk about me as an infant crawling around this house following Big Mama hoping she would feed me one of the treats I enjoyed eating, particularly my favorite: biscuits and gravy. Big Mama interrupted the storytelling by announcing loudly, "Breakfast is ready, everybody!" The wonderful aromas of freshly baked biscuits, sausage, bacon, scrambled eggs, and buttered grits overpowered my senses. An additional two folding tables, draped with white tablecloths, and extra chairs had been set up to accommodate us all. Big Mama helped us as we served ourselves, buffet-style. When I took my plate to the table, my mouth watering, I noticed a pot of homemade strawberry jam. Once we were all seated, Big Mama said grace, and then we all proceeded to devour as much food as possible. The biscuits seem to melt in my mouth. We ate everything; when we were done, we helped clean the kitchen. Big Mama wanted everyone to take a nap so we slept on the floor. When we awoke, Big Mama was holding two large bags of clothes for us to try on. Everyone got to take a bath and dressed into one of the outfits from the bags of clothes.

It was after two in the afternoon. Big Mama announced that we were going to the family July fourth celebration, so we crowded into two cars—a 1957 Buick Century driven by my granddaddy, and a 1962 Chevy Impala driven by Big Mama. Soon we all arrived at a large gathering of big Momma's family, including her mother, father and other siblings, nieces, nephews and cousins. Food was everywhere, inside and outside, and the backyard covered at least two acres. The kids were busy playing, but I helped myself to delicacies such as fried chicken, catfish, pork chops, deviled eggs, potato salad, coleslaw, macaroni and cheese, and collard greens. Of course, there was plenty of watermelon, and a delightful version of my favorite dessert, pecan pie. Finally, dusk arrived, marking the beginning of many fireworks displays. At the end of the night, everyone went home completely content thanks to wonderful food and family.

The next day, another miracle occurred. After breakfast, Big Mama faced a busy day: getting us additional clothing, registering us for vacation Bible school, obtaining bunk beds for the rooms, and completing paperwork for securing custody of us (a formality, but necessary). Just as she started to leave, a long-distance phone call from Cushing Academy required my grandparents' immediate attention. They entered their bedroom, closed the door, and talked on the phone for about fifteen minutes. Then they emerged from their bedroom, smiling, and asked me to come to the phone.

A voice introduced himself as the Dean of Students at Cushing Academy. "May I call you Jim?"

I answered, "Yes, sir."

"Jim, we would love to have you as one of our students this fall to begin the ninth grade. Your academic performance has been superb, as well as your aptitude test scores. We feel that you will do fine to start this fall without going to summer school. How do you feel about this opportunity?"

I was briefly stunned by what I had just heard and was speechless for a couple of seconds before I gathered my thoughts. Then I blurted, "Oh my goodness! Wow! Yes, I would love to begin ninth grade at Cushing Academy!"

The dean continued, "We understand that your mother would not give her permission for you to attend Cushing. Would it cause a problem in your mind if your grandparents permitted you to come?"

I laughed, "No problem at all, sir! Thank you so much for this opportunity!" I paused. "If I may ask …where is Cushing Academy?"

"Jim, we are located near the New Hampshire border in central Massachusetts," he replied. "We are about sixty miles west of Boston. We will be sending you and your grandparents an admission packet containing information regarding what to wear, travel directions to reach us, and consent forms for your grandparents to sign. Please make sure they return the signed consent forms to us thirty days prior to beginning of classes. Again Jim, congratulations and welcome to Cushing Academy!"

I couldn't stop grinning. "Thank you, sir!" I took a deep breath and continued, "But, sir, my grandparents cannot afford to pay anything. How much does tuition cost?"

The dean said, "You will be on scholarship. All of your expenses will be paid from a scholarship fund established for bright, deserving students like you. All of this information will be included in the admissions packet we will be sending to you. You will need to pay for your transportation, however. I hope that's not a problem, but in case it is let us know and we will see what can be done, okay?"

"Yes, sir," I said, nodding briskly, "thank you so much, sir! You don't know what this means to me! I am so excited to come to Cushing."

I heard him chuckle. "Very well, Jim. Now let me speak to your grandparents again." I passed the phone to Big Mama. She talked an additional few seconds before she hung up the phone. When she turned to face me with one of those smiles that could light up any room or place, a feeling of love washed over me.

"Well, Van, what do you think, honey?" she asked.

I raised my arms and shouted, "I am going to Cushing Academy!" Big Mama, Granddaddy, and I embraced. Very quickly my brothers and sisters joined us in one large embrace with me in the middle. Tears of joy rolled down my face. Those same feelings I experienced years ago in my backyard, feeling special, chosen, serene—those feelings recurred. Yes, indeed, a miracle happened. I had been given a second chance; my hopes and dreams had been resurrected. I closed my eyes and began to hear the voice of my eight-grade history teacher reciting the same words of encouragement that he did at the end of every history class: *Young Negro boy, what will you do when time makes you a man? Will you miss the mark or fight to hold your stand?* Those words would become my mantra. I imagined that I was that young boy and that I would make the mark! This opportunity would be the wind in my sails.

CHAPTER 2

Cushing Years

ummer sped by; I was anxious to embark upon my journey to Cushing. Big Mama took me shopping at Sears, which was a big deal for me. I was used to hand-me-downs and thrift-store clothes. We purchased two sports coats, three pairs of slacks, three white shirts, one pair of penny loafers, three pairs of socks, and some underwear. Boy, new Sears clothing. I was as proud as a peacock! I owned more clothing now than I ever had, and yet all of my belongings fit into one suitcase.

September 7, 1965, marked the beginning of my journey to fulfill my dream. I boarded a Trailways bus, waved goodbye to my grandparents, brothers, and sisters, then began my thirty-six-hour odyssey to Ashburnham, Massachusetts. The itinerary mailed to me stated that I would be picked up by the Dean of Students, Mr. Leyden. The air on the bus was thick with cigarette smoke, and the stench permeated my new clothing—how dreadful! Still, I managed to nap periodically. When awake, I enjoyed the passing scenery of cities, towns, and farms. The bus made brief stops, but I did not have much of an appetite and basically survived on liquids the entire trip. We traveled through Washington, D.C., Philadelphia, and New York City. I was overwhelmed by the size of New York City. I changed buses in New York City, then it was on to Boston

Massachusetts. From Boston charter service bus took me through Worcester, Massachusetts, then on to Fitchburg and Gardner, Massachusetts. I was nervous upon arriving at my destination as I was about to meet the Leyden family. As I disembarked from the bus the Leyden family was there and greeted me immediately. As I was about to take the final step forward to reach the ground, my penny loafer penny with it's image of Abraham Lincoln, glistened from the bright lights reflecting off of it. The Leydens greeted me with a smile and welcomed me to Massachusetts. I was shaking their hands when all of a sudden their little boy, who was no more than five years old, shouted, "Mommy, Daddy! That's a Negro!"

I smiled. Mr. and Mrs. Leyden replied, "Yes, son, you're right," and they smiled too. Then Mr. Leyden asked, "Was the bus ride tolerable?"

I replied, "Yes, sir."

"Well, let's get your luggage and drive to Cushing," he said. "It's getting late and you'll need your rest, as tomorrow is a busy day." After we retrieved my single suitcase, then all of us drove to Ashburnham, where Cushing Academy was located (approximately ten miles away). Once on campus, we drove to the freshman boys' dormitory. It was after ten. I briefly met the dormitory Master (a faculty member) and student Prefect (a senior student). My roommate introduced himself and made me feel welcome. He was much taller than I, appearing to be well over six feet tall. He was starting his sophomore year. I was a scrawny 5'4" weakling! Man, was I intimidated! My roommate quickly explained some of the rules before we both retired to our respective beds for the night.

Morning came quickly. Everyone rushed to get showered, shaved (those of us with facial hair), and dressed by seven o'clock. Then everyone walked to the dining hall for breakfast. The early sunlight revealed lush green lawns and manicured shrubbery. Pine trees as well as deciduous trees loomed everywhere. Fall's colorful foliage display had just begun.

French doors framed the dining hall entrance; the hall itself had extensive wood molding and wood-paneled walls. The tables all had linen tablecloths and beautiful china settings for six to ten people. A teacher or administrator sat at the head of each table. No one sat until a bell rang; then, students waiters carried large trays of food to each table.

After twenty minutes, the bell rang, and everyone got up to leave. Another group of students waited, lined up at the dining room entry. It was then that I noticed that all of the boys and men had shirts, ties, and sport coats on; girls and women wore dresses or skirts (even miniskirts). I felt self-conscious about my Sears clothes; their clothes appeared very expensive and well-made. It was that moment that I realized the extent of wealth associated with the students and the school.

Mr. Leyden had been right: my day was incredibly busy. I went through orientation then started classes: English, math, science, history, and foreign language (French). Prior to dinner, chores were assigned, which included assignments for grounds work, raking leaves, kitchen service, and waiter duties. After chores, we went to mandatory physical educations, i.e., organized sports. Football for boys and field hockey for girls were sports for the fall season. Winter sports included swimming, basketball, and ice hockey, and in the spring we would choose from track and field, tennis, baseball, and softball. I chose football as my fall sport. I wanted to be a jock; I thought jocks were popular and beloved. I was small, so I wanted to convey the image of toughness. To gain approval, I was never afraid of physical confrontation on the sports field. I quickly earned the nickname, "Tennessee Toughie." After sports, it was time for dinner, followed by a social hour, an opportunity to get to know other students. Cushing Academy was one of only a few co-ed private schools in New England at that time. It seemed to me that a more natural environment was created by having girls present, and that that environment would better prepare me for the real world. I believed very early in my life that women were at least man's equal. I made friends with a small group of guys and girls. We enjoyed each other's company and studied together whenever possible.

At the end of the day, boys and girls returned to their respective dorms. Quiet time and study hall lasted until ten. Students could request to stay up an additional hour to study or finish homework, but then it was lights out and to bed. Each day during the week was a carbon copy. Weekends were devoted to scheduled sports games against neighboring prep schools and, rarely, junior-college teams. We also had dances, movie nights, concerts, and plays. Sundays were slower paced but always began with chapel service following breakfast. Sunday was also visitation day for family and friends, plus students who had gone home (weekends off campus) returned on Sunday. Since I was too poor to travel home for every holiday, I was often invited to go home with friends or roommate—especially for long weekends and Thanksgiving. I was always grateful for the offer as well as the opportunity to get to know someone and their family better.

During the first year, I was pleasantly surprised by how well I performed academically. I was extremely well-prepared by the advanced curriculum in the eighth grade in Richmond. I made the honor roll the entire first year and every year thereafter. I attracted a lot of attention from faculty and students as a result. I could almost hear them thinking, *How could this poor black boy from Tennessee be so well prepared and smart?* Comments like, "You are a credit to your race," and, "You deserve all the breaks you get," were common from both faculty and students. By the end of the first school year, I felt genuinely welcomed and assimilated, as though I had transcended race. And, once I arrived home, my family greeted me like a hero. A tradition started upon my return every summer. I had to run the gauntlet: that is, my four brothers formed a line that I had to successfully pass in order to reach the front door. Victor, Michael, Julius, and David tried their best to keep me from reaching the front door. However, I was much stronger and larger so I usually prevailed. As nice as Cushing was, it was good to be home with Granddaddy and Big Mama and my siblings.

Big Mama was the head cook and dietitian for Chattanooga city schools, which allowed her to develop friendships with influential public figures. She made some phone calls and was able to secure a summer job for me working for the city of Chattanooga cleaning vacant lots. The job paid $1.60 per hour. I worked ten weeks, saving most of the money to use for clothing and incidental expenses at Cushing. I was able to purchase two sport coats, slacks, new shoes, socks, and ties. Additionally, I paid for my travel expenses. Although the summer went by quickly, I did manage to get up to date with my brothers' and sisters' lives, and it was always good to talk with Granddaddy. He was always so calm, knowledgeable, and reassuring. He had a regal air about him. As he puffed on a cigar, his long, flowing white hair created a striking resemblance to Colonel Sanders of Kentucky Fried Chicken fame. I often asked him about his heritage but he was always evasive about specifics. He would only say that his dad was from the Middle East. Some years later, Big Mama privately gave me more information about Granddaddy's heritage. He was born to a single mom in the 1890s which was considered taboo. He was always very ashamed of this fact and preferred not to talk about it. My sister Janice became the family records keeper and heritage investigator years later. She found pictures of our grandfather and his mother standing in front of the apartment they lived in, which sat on top of a Jewish store. She discovered that they were descendants of the family that owned the store. Hopefully, we all will learn the truth about the family name one day, because both Big Mama and Granddaddy took that secret to the grave. Still, I love them both dearly and thought of both of them as my parents. Both were always encouraging and proud of my achievements.

Summer ended, and again I traveled to Cushing by bus. It was the start of my sophomore year. I was assigned a new roommate from upstate New York. We both were assigned to a new dorm. The guys in this dorm were really materialistic, typical teenagers. They were into cars, clothes, and girls. I was considered a nerd because my priorities were different. My roommate and others in the dorm constantly criticized my clothes. They were quick to point out their Brooks Brothers clothing labels. However, after the first grading period when they received Cs and Ds, and I received straight As, all of a sudden, everyone wanted to be my friend. During my first year at Cushing, there were fewer than ten African American students present. To my surprise, an additional ten African American students enrolled at the beginning of my sophomore year. I was elated to have more black students present at Cushing. Most were from a similar economic background to mine, which made me feel somewhat more comfortable. I must admit that I was intimidated by the large economic and social differences between me and the rest of the students. The group of black students all got to know each other well, and in many cases were roommates. We helped make the boring social hour more exciting with Motown music, dancing, and card games. I loved partnering in cards with a guy named Haff from Cleveland, Ohio. He was one of the most gregarious and entertaining personalities I have ever had the privilege to know. I often wish I had remained in contact with him. All of the African American boys were superb athletes, quickly becoming campus heroes. I was not as talented but at least I tried hard, and did become good enough to make the varsity teams my senior year.

The other noteworthy event to occur during my sophomore year was my keen interest in girls. I developed a crush on a pretty young lady named Penny. I let it be known by friends that I was interested and discovered that she felt the same about me. Penny and I dated during the last half of my sophomore year. She was my first real girlfriend, and my crush turned into something deeper. We spent hours together, getting to know each other. We went to dances and other social events as a couple. After social hour, the evening would end with an embrace and kiss beneath a tree on campus, a location that has become something of a tradition for couples at Cushing. Just before the end of the school year, the relationship terminated abruptly (I still don't know why). Although before parting for our respective homes and summer, we wished each other well.

Summer started at home upon my arrival with the traditional gauntlet run to enter the house. It was wonderful to return home and to Big Mama's cooking. Big Mama was also able to find employment for me with Olan Mills, a photography business. I was employed as an assistant to one of the main photographers. In fact, I was fortunate to remain employed by Olan Mills for the remaining summers I spent at home for the next three years. My evenings and weekends were devoted to family gatherings and outdoor cooking and games. Most of the time, we played softball or basketball, usually on a dry, dusty field. The basketball hoop was a bottomless fruit basket nailed to a tree. Imagine playing basketball in ninety-five-degree summer heat with dust flying everywhere! Sundays were devoted to church and eating some of the most mouthwatering foods I have ever tasted. Gosh did I love being home those summers!

The summer of 1967 ended and I was off to Cushing to start my junior year. This time I flew back to Cushing. The airline industry had begun to offer huge student discounts, so I took advantage of the lower fares, which had become competitive with long-distance bus travel. Air travel remained a luxury in 1967. The attendants treated everyone as though they were first-class passengers. There were no crowds, luggage arrived on time every time, and even the food served was good. Airlines in those days were extremely customer service committed. For example, on one of my trips home, we departed from Boston as usual and started the short flight to New York City's LaGuardia

Airport. From there, I usually changed planes for the flight to Chattanooga. However, weather events diverted my plane to JFK airport in New York. Without delay, the airline provided a helicopter to fly us from JFK to the top of the Pan Am building in Manhattan, from which we proceeded to LaGuardia via chartered bus. We all made the connecting LaGuardia flight on time! Those were the good old days of air travel. It was refreshing to arrive at my destination in three hours rather than the thirty-six required for bus travel. Additionally, I did not smell like a smoke stack.

I had great anticipation for my junior year. I was an upperclassman, on the honor roll, and well-liked by all on campus. I started to develop a mindset of invincibility: I was young, strong, gifted, and black … it was my time. During the summer, I had undergone a tremendous growth spurt, growing five inches and gaining fifteen pounds. I was described as tall and handsome, but not quite the 6'2" I was hoping to be to impress Penny. I had not gotten over her all summer. Back at school she appeared to avoid me, and when I did manage to talk with her, I knew we were done as a couple. She quickly found a new boyfriend on campus, much to my dismay. I simply could not understand how someone could reject me! Tall, handsome, honor roll: big man on campus! The more mature side of me took over, however, and reminded me of the real reason I was at Cushing. I could not afford to lose sight of my dream; I even fantasized about winning the Nobel Prize for my contributions to science. I wanted my life to make a difference, to be an upstanding, contributing citizen—not a black citizen, just an American citizen. I felt that I was part of that quiet revolution occurring in America of educated, talented African Americans being assimilated into mainstream America. I became a man on a mission. I buried myself in my studies and earned induction into the cum laude honors society and school honor-roll society; I also joined both the history and chess clubs. I enjoyed my best year on the football and basketball teams and was a strong competitor on the track team as well. Overall, I was extremely pleased with the first half of the year.

However, I also ignored a changing world, a world of confrontational politics. The Black Power movement arrived on campus during the fall and winter terms. Several of the African American students returned from summer break with Afros. An air of tension permeated the campus. Arguments broke out between black and white students. I recall one dismayed student saying to me, "You guys are always happy and smiling; so what's wrong?" Well, what was wrong manifested itself in the riots in Detroit and Watts. The assassination of Dr. King made matters worse. There were divisions even among the African American students. Some of us, myself included, were criticized for being too conservative and naïve enough to think that a good education represented the only necessity for inclusion in mainstream America. This accusation stunned me, because I firmly believed that the opportunity given to us to attend an excellent prep school and receive an A+ education was the ticket to a better life. However, what if I was wrong? Could all of this urban turmoil truly have come to pass because people realized the utter hopelessness facing them, no matter how much they tried assimilating into mainstream society? A rage, a swell of anger started to boil within me. Maybe the black militants were right. Maybe it was time for a new day, a new beginning, a revolution.

In spite of all the uneasiness, at the end of the day, we were all human beings with feelings and emotions. We all needed human touch and validation. I had the distinct honor of a spring romance with Joan. We were both honors students, high achievers. Emotionally, she was far more mature than I. She taught me how to feel deeply, to reach out and touch, and to allow myself to be touched. We found refuge in each other's arms, temporarily escaping all of the turmoil surrounding us. We truly enjoyed each other's company. Our evenings always ended under Lovers' Tree with an intimate kiss and hug.

Different social strata, different races, different philosophies united to confirm that love conquers all. We both hated for the school year to end, since we have to part for the summer. I often read what she wrote in my yearbook even to this day. The words, like her voice, soothe me: "Jim, words seem so meaningless at moments like this. These past few days have been some of the most wonderful I've ever spent. You've made me happier than I've ever been. Although, physically, we won't be together this summer, we will continue to share the feelings we have for each other in our hearts until next fall and then … all my love, Joan. P.S. 'Tiger! Tiger! burning bright / In the forests of the night / What immortal hand or eye / Could frame thy fearful symmetry?'" I floated into the summer with high hopes that she was the one.

All summer, my thoughts turned to Joan. I had sent her a dozen beautiful yellow roses with a romantic letter within one week of arriving home for the summer. She never answered my letter, nor was I sure that she had received the roses I sent to her. I was heartbroken as thoughts of rejection again filled my mind. I reminded myself to stay positive and not think the worst. Hopefully, she was well. Finally, September arrived— and I returned to school as a senior! Maybe I could rekindle my relationship with Joan. Then, as plain as day I received a harsh dose of reality. There she was, walking toward me with someone else by her side. His arm was around her waist, leaving no doubt about their relationship. Later that day, she approached me and confirmed what I suspected. We embraced, said our goodbyes, and vowed to remain friends. I swallowed my pride and devoted my energy and thoughts to finishing my senior year strong academically and gaining admission to college.

I had taken the SAT exam during my junior year, but I decided to retake it to improve my score. College visitations and interviews were starting. I decided that to continue the pursuit of my dream, I needed to attend an engineering college to major in science or engineering. Worcester Polytechnic Institute, located only a couple of hours away in central Massachusetts, invited me to an early interview at the very start of my senior year. The interview went extremely well; I was offered early admission, and if I accepted, I could not accept any other college admissions offers. Of course, admission was contingent upon successful completion of my senior year—not a problem or obstacle for me. It was October and I had been admitted to college, with a full scholarship for four years!

WPI was touted as exceptional, an excellent undergraduate engineering college. I was told that I was only the second Cushing graduate accepted for admission to this highly competitive university. The core curriculum was rigorous, and included required physics and advanced calculus courses for the first two years! However, I felt that my Cushing education had prepared me well. I also received good news regarding my SAT score, which I'd managed to raise to 1200 out of a possible 1600. Academically things were going so well that I decided that I didn't need to study as hard the rest of the year. This attitude proved disastrous as I earned my first F ever! Thankfully, the grade was preliminary as it only covered the first six weeks of my calculus course. The teacher reprimanded me for not doing my best. He warned me to improve or I would have to drop the course. I quickly got the message and responded with all As on all homework and tests. By the end of the first semester I had raised my grade to a B. My teacher continued to challenge me with extra homework assignments. His exams seemed to become more difficult but I seemed to rise to the occasion and excelled, finally receiving all As in calculus the remainder of the year—I even won the class prize for the best calculus student. They awarded me a book containing well-known math conundrums, some unsolved (*Famous Problems Of Mathematics* by Heinrich Tietze). One of the unsolved problems was Fermat's last theorem, for which the publisher offered a cash prize for its solution. I never solved the problem, nor did anyone else until recently.

At graduation I received another special acknowledgment: the Schoolboy Award for academic excellence all four years at Cushing. Prior to graduation, I was invited to speak in Boston at a gathering of concerned students addressing the social issues of the day, and possible solutions. I was the voice of moderation, supporting social change by working within society rather than separating from it. We all had the feeling that soon it would be our time, and that we could bring real change to improve society.

I left Cushing as a well-educated young man, tolerant, and understanding of differences, as were many friends I had at school. Our experiences were invaluable, teaching all of us to respect each other and to go out into the world to share that respect for others.

The summer of 1969 was quiet in Chattanooga. I worked for Olan Mills again as a photographer assistant. I was glad to have the job, which enabled me to save money for my first semester of college. My clothing bill would be far less expensive because I would not need the dressy clothes I wore at Cushing; college did not have a dress code.

Mom had moved to Chattanooga and tried to reclaim all of us; however, my brothers and sisters refused. I decided to live with Mom to help her out. However, her behavior became very strange as the summer progressed. Near the end of summer, she started to hear voices and hallucinate. One day I walked in on her burning the Bible! I knew it would not be long before she had to be placed into a mental hospital again. I cried myself to sleep that night.

The time was drawing near for my departure to WPI to commence my freshman year. Everyone at my job was excited for me. The secretary working in the office was an attractive woman in her mid-to-late thirties. She greeted everyone with a smile. We talked as often as time permitted during the summer. She was most excited for me to have the opportunity to attend college and encouraged me to make the most of it. She thought that I would have a bright future. One day, we were left in the office alone during the lunch hour. We talked about a wide range of subjects and expressed our mutual fondness for each other. Our eyes locked and soon we were kissing passionately. We quickly moved to a more private location and proceeded with more kissing and fondling. We decided to meet privately. However, I could not follow through. I was nervous and felt that an experienced older woman was out of my league. We continued our make-out sessions, however, during the last few days I was in Chattanooga. I accepted her phone number and promised to keep in touch once I arrived at school. I was confused but flattered by her attention.

CHAPTER 3

College Years

I arrived at Worcester Polytechnic Institute the first week of September 1969. The first women were admitted to WPI in my freshman class, along with the school's largest ever number of African American students. There was a feeling of excitement on campus, as the United States had landed a man on the moon, and returned him and his fellow astronauts back to Earth safely. In terms of popular culture, Woodstock was still fresh in everyone's mind; around every corner, it seemed you could find musicians playing amid the smoke from marijuana. My first day on campus was most embarrassing. Nearly everyone appeared to be dressed in counterculture hippie clothing; most of the black students were sporting Afros. I quickly found a store near campus and purchased a couple of pairs of bell-bottom jeans and some tie-dyed T-shirts. I did not want to look like a nerd; I wanted to fit in. It would take some time for my hair to grow into an Afro, but maybe I could invent some reason for having short hair. You could spot the real nerds a mile away because of the slide rules hanging from their belts.

I had to get used to all the freedom of college. There was no one to make me go to class or study. There was always some social gathering or party to go to, not only on campus, but also at neighboring colleges in Worcester and in Boston if one could arrange transportation. Every Tuesday evening, female students from neighboring all-girls colleges were bused onto our campus for social events. This practice continued even after WPI became coed.

The very first Tuesday evening, I met my future wife Brenda. Of course, when we first met I didn't know we would marry one day, but I had a special feeling about her from the very beginning. She was tall, beautiful, and gifted, having graduated as the salutatorian of her class. We were both southerners, so we felt comfortable together. Although I was intent on remaining single and not become committed to anyone so soon, I felt drawn to her, and it wasn't long before we were dating exclusively.

College campuses were in turmoil all over the country, especially in New England and the northeast. Antiwar fever was high; protest marches against the Vietnam War occurred almost every weekend. Additionally, the civil rights movement and Black Power movements were conducting their own protest marches. Civil disobedience was the order of the day. There were protests, sit-ins, and numerous takeovers of college campus buildings. Brenda and I shared the same convictions and participated in numerous civil rights and antiwar demonstrations. Many black students also protested the lack of African American studies courses at the colleges they attended. At WPI, we lobbied for separate living quarters. Our argument was that African American students living together would foster an enhanced atmosphere of pride, nurturing, and academic achievement. The administration approved this concept, so all of the black students at WPI were allowed to occupy the entire floor of a brand-new dormitory; the black female students lived together in their own section of the designated female dorm. We all socialized together. For the first time in my life I drank alcohol, usually beer and wine. Marijuana was widely available, and I experimented with it also.

By Thanksgiving, Brenda and I were seriously in love. She

invited me to her home for Christmas to meet her family, and I accepted. She was the fifth of six siblings. Her oldest sister still lived at home. She was well-educated, witty, highly intelligent, beautiful, and most gracious—a schoolteacher and single with a very active social life when she was not working or taking care of matters at home. The oldest child, one of Brenda's brothers, lived in California; another brother lived nearby. The third brother had recently graduated from college and worked in business. Brenda's mother and father were so kind and gracious to me, I immediately felt very comfortable and welcomed to their home.

I was reluctant to leave when the time came for me to travel home to Chattanooga for the remainder of the Christmas holiday. I was sure that Brenda would become my wife, so I did not want to leave her side. When I arrived home, I expressed my love for Brenda to my grandparents, brothers, and sisters. The adults cautioned me to be patient and finish my education before I married, which made sense to me.

I returned to college a couple of days ahead of Brenda going back to Anna Maria College. First semester grades were available and for the first time in my life I did not make the honor roll! Brenda did not meet her expectations academically either. We both promised to devote more of our time to academics and studying. We tried hard but by the end of the second semester we both had not improved our GPAs. I was highly disappointed and so was she. In fact, Brenda had fared worse than I. She would have to attend summer school in order to maintain her scholarship, which meant remaining at Anna Maria for six weeks to repeat two courses. She also decided to change her major from medical lab technology to education. She decided to become a teacher like her sister. We kept in touch; I think I wrote to her and she wrote to me at least two to three times a week. She successfully completed summer school, maintained her scholarship, and raised her GPA significantly.

I was delighted to feel her in my arms again when she arrived home from summer school.

While Brenda was in summer school, I got a job at a large chemical factory near my grandparents' neighborhood. It was a great summer job for a chemistry major. The job description included performing errands, keeping chemical stocks supplied for the staff, and cleaning the plant. I was paid significantly more than my previous summer job, so I was able to save money, give my grandparents money to help with expenses, and gain valuable work experience and insight regarding the commercial chemistry industry.

I also traveled to see Brenda in Birmingham nearly every weekend that I could, usually every other weekend. Her mom was a great cook! Her dad was quiet and reserved, but always gave me the look of approval. Brenda's youngest sister, the baby of the family, was also a joy. I thought that the jovial welcome I had received from her during Christmas holiday was just because she wanted me to feel welcome to her home. However, it turned out she was always jovial, playful, and most entertaining—which I suspected she did mostly to irritate Brenda. Some good old sibling rivalry, I guess.

Brenda had numerous relatives living near and around Birmingham, and I think I met them all that summer. The weekends were always festive affairs with friends, family, and great food. Sooner than either of us wished, it was time to return to school.

Brenda and I returned to college as a solid couple. We felt committed to each other. I loved her and she loved me. To our delight, more African American students had been admitted to our respective colleges. We all felt the need to nurture each other, to be supportive, to make life on campus as hospitable as possible. Collectively we decided to establish a Black Student Union on campus. We socialized together, studied together, and lived together, and supported each other day in and day out. Thanks to that support, I finally made the honor roll after the first semester. I was proud of this accomplishment and so were my black brothers and sisters.

The curriculum at WPI was extremely demanding, claiming over two hundred of my freshman classmates by the end of the freshman year, so I felt even prouder that I had succeeded. Black pride and nationalism were sweeping the country, especially on college campuses. Antiwar sentiment continued to spread; it seemed that many college students believed it would take a revolution to effect the kind of social change sought by the radical left and Black Power movement. The Black Panthers, Weathermen, Socialists, and quasi-communist groups were frequent visitors to college campuses to recruit, particularly in the Northeast and on the West Coast. They often sought science and engineering students for their technical expertise. I attended and listened at many of their meetings, searching long and deep within me: was I willing to commit to a cause that advocated violence and killing as a means to an end? Brenda and I discussed these matters many times with other students. She and I, as well as a few of our friends, decided to dedicate our education and our lives to achieving change by becoming part of the system, effecting change from within.

That year, I was elected president of the Black Student Union. I quickly developed a reputation as the voice of moderation, of inclusion rather than exclusion. I became a liaison between students and the administration. In retrospect, I think those of us who believed in this philosophy may have prevented drastic measures, such as student takeover of administration buildings on campus, which was contrary to what was happening on the other college campuses. The Black Student Union decided to reach out to help the poor, hungry, and needy in the city of Worcester. We decided to collect clothing and food for delivery by Thanksgiving as a way of giving back to the community. Our group received broad support from the faculty and students at WPI, even receiving favorable coverage by the news media.

The program was so successful that we decided to make it a tradition every Thanksgiving.

The faculty and administration also appointed me as student representative to the Trustees committee—a very important position. Still, as busy as I was, I decided to try out for the college basketball team. To my surprise, I made the team! The coach worked us hard with extensive conditioning drills and scrimmages, usually lasting to near ten at night, which left little time for studying. I was even too fatigued to attend my classes regularly. In fact, my priorities had slowly changed from studying to serving as a goodwill ambassador on campus. I attended lots of meetings on campus and at other surrounding colleges, while weekends were devoted to spending time with Brenda and playing in scheduled basketball games, some of which were off campus.

By the end of my sophomore year, my GPA took a nose-dive. I was shocked at how poorly I had done, so I made a decision to rededicate myself to my studies. I left the basketball team and attended fewer meetings, and Brenda and I agreed not to see each other every Tuesday evening so that I could study. My grades did improve, but I wanted to return to the honor roll. I pondered what else I needed to do to accomplish this. I loved Brenda, but was I seeing her too much? Should we stop dating? Individuals I confided in, both faculty and students, encouraged me to stay balanced, to have a life outside of the classroom. I took their advice, but it was difficult; my curriculum was brutal. I was required to successfully complete two years of science and math courses, which included two years of physics and two years of calculus. Still, I soldiered on.

My college advisor recommended two things to me at the end of my sophomore year. He felt that I had excellent people skills; he could not picture me as a scientist confined to the lab. He felt that I should consider taking additional liberal arts courses in order to consider a career in medicine. By 1970 to 1971, a severe economic retraction had begun, and the demand for scientists and engineers faltered as a result. Major employers, including NASA and Boeing, were downsizing and laying off thousands. My advisor thought that I should consider applying to medical school. He informed me that there was a shortage of doctors nationally, and medical schools were starting to admit larger numbers of applicants who had majored in science, math, and engineering. He told me a story about one of his friends who was a science major and decide to become a doctor. His friend became a radiologist and developed a busy practice covering three states, which he covered by flying his own personal airplane! I became intrigued and excited by this opportunity. My science background would be of considerable help mastering the basic science requirements of medical school, and my physics background would be invaluable to a specialty in radiology. I envisioned saving thousands upon thousands of lives! It made me feel good to contribute to humanity and advance health care in this country. I made the necessary changes to my course of study, declaring a major in chemistry with minors in biochemistry and biomedical sciences.

The second semester at WPI ended quietly, while chaos continued to occur all around us. The antiwar movement was becoming institutionalized. The death and corruption occurring in Vietnam had reached America. News of the My Lai massacre had infuriated the public. Students had been killed at Kent State the previous spring. Soon, the Pentagon Papers would become public knowledge and reveal the true nature of the Vietnam War: drug trafficking, political assassinations, and indiscriminate bombings. I couldn't take it all; I was ready for summer.

The summer of 1971 started with the usual job-search in Chattanooga. This time, I was fortunate to find a job with a factory that manufactored pipe for industrial use. The job paid well—in fact, it was my best-paying job ever. I worked the graveyard shift, which took a while for me to adapt to, but after two weeks I had acclimated. Unfortunately, it seemed that as soon as I had gotten comfortable and in a routine, turmoil found me.

Granddaddy and Big Mama wanted to meet Brenda's family, so we all traveled to Birmingham and had a great reception. I had not informed my grandparents yet about my plans to become engaged to Brenda, but they seemed to sense that I was very serious about her; I am sure they discussed it with her parents. Less than two weeks after their meeting, however, Brenda discovered that she was pregnant! She didn't tell me about the situation until I arrived in Birmingham for my weekend visit. I can't describe in words the fear and anxiety that overtook me; I sensed that Brenda had similar feelings. Her parents took Brenda and me for a car ride for private discussion.

Brenda's mom did all of the talking. She voiced a series of rapid questions, repeating one over and over: "Jimmy, what are you going to do about this?"

Once I got a chance to respond I said, as calmly as I could, "I'm going to get a job and work."

Brenda's mom responded, "That will ruin your life—and Brenda's too!" I didn't know what to say.

When we got home, the mood was grim. This was undoubtedly a low point in our relationship. The bus ride back to Chattanooga seemed longer than usual. I didn't want Brenda to get an abortion, but we were not ready for a family so soon, either. As soon as I got home, Brenda called and asked me to send money for an abortion. The request took my breath away. I could not believe that a decision had been made so quickly. I agreed to send the money as soon as I could, which I did five days later. Shortly thereafter, I received another phone call from Brenda's mom. She informed me that Brenda was ill and had been hospitalized! She reassured me that she was going to be okay, and that I should come see her by the end of the week. I arrived in Birmingham that Saturday morning, and immediately was taken to the hospital. I was so glad to see her. We embraced each other for a long time.

"What happened?" I asked.

She sighed, "I got the abortion and developed complications which caused me to get appendicitis. But my doctor said I'll be okay." I gave her a long embrace and a kiss. I promised that I would never leave her. We both cried; we had lost our first child. Now more than ever, I knew that she would become my wife very soon.

I arrived back in Chattanooga with renewed focus: I needed to save as much money as possible. I decided to ask Brenda's parents for her hand in marriage. I would present her with the engagement ring by Christmas, I thought to myself. I had just finished this thought when my grandparents confronted me. Big Mama did all the talking, asking me to give them half of my earnings every week in order to remain at home. I was stunned, and of course I wanted to know why. She said that I was an adult now, and I needed to move out.

Oh my God! I thought to myself, *I am being kicked out*! I would need all of my earnings to help pay for college expenses. The full scholarship from WPI had been modified at the end of my sophomore year so that my junior and senior years would be paid for by student loans rather than grant money. I would be responsible for my books, clothing, travel, and laundry expenses, as well as any discretionary income. I was hurt and angry. I had no place to go. However, I was determined to show them that I could survive on my own, so I left with nothing but the clothes on my back. I walked out into the night, not immediately knowing my destination. I looked back and saw my brothers and sisters standing in the doorway, waving goodbye. I kept walking, turning my head to look forward. With tears streaming down my face and clenched fists, I promised myself that I would make it. *I'll show them!* I thought, over and over.

I can't explain it but somehow I ended up in a neighborhood near the house where my mother had stayed the previous summer. It looked abandoned at first, but I spotted a dim light. *What should I do?* I thought to myself. What if she wasn't there? I did not relish the thought of sleeping outside, so I knocked on the front door several times. It opened slowly and there stood my mom.

I took a deep breath. "Mom, I need a place to stay. Can you help me?"

She hugged me and started to cry, saying, "Of course you can stay here with me, baby!"

I hugged her also, and then released her. I had to ask, "Mom, are you okay?"

"Yes baby, I was released from the mental hospital six months ago," she replied. "No one seems to want me around, so I live here by myself. Come on and tell me how school is going." She took my hand and led me inside.

My mom sounded good. She made sense when she talked. *Maybe she is well now, and we can be a family again.* So I said, "Actually, school is going well. I'll be a junior when I return this fall, majoring in chemistry, and I want to go to medical school to become a doctor."

Mom replied, "Oh, how wonderful, honey! You can become a doctor like me!" I wasn't sure what she meant, but at the time I shrugged it off. She continued, "Let's get something to eat; you look like you could use a good meal!"

Dinner was meager but welcome; I inhaled it! When I was finished, Mom smiled at me. "Now honey, you get your rest. You need to go to work in the morning, right?"

I shook my head. "I work the night shift, so I try to sleep during the day."

"Well, you're welcome to stay here. I'm off to bed, but I'll see you in the morning." With that, she headed off to her room. The two-bedroom wood-frame house was sparsely furnished: Mom's bed, two folding chairs in the front area, two chairs and a small table in the kitchen area, and that was it. I found myself a corner on the floor and fell asleep, happy that I did not have to sleep outside.

I must've slept more than ten hours before I awoke in a sunbeam. It was summer and hot. There was no air conditioning; I was sweaty and sticky, so I got up to bathe. I thought I heard someone talking on the porch off the kitchen so I looked out the window and saw only Mom. Immediately I grew sad; I had hoped that she was better or even well, but she was talking to herself, gesticulating wildly. I thought to myself that it was the Lord's will for me to be here at this time to help take care of her. When I left to go to work at ten o'clock that night, Mom had spent nearly the entire day talking and cursing at an imaginary something or someone. There were brief periods of quiet that would end with a loud thud. I later discovered that sound was the Bible hitting the wall after she had thrown it. This pattern repeated itself nearly every day. I purchased groceries and gave her money to help out with expenses such as rent and utilities, and I prayed for her recovery. My refuges were the weekend trips to see Brenda in Birmingham.

Near the end of the summer, after returning from a weekend trip to Birmingham, I smelled smoke as I entered the house. I panicked; I ran through the house yelling, "Mom, where are you?"

A voice came from the back yard. "I'm here, honey, outside." I quickly ran to the back yard. There was mom standing over a burning Bible. She just stared off into the distance, not speaking a word. I was speechless. After several minutes had passed, I asked quietly, "Why are you burning a Bible?" She did not answer me.

Ten days later, I returned to Massachusetts.

The refreshing crisp fall air of Massachusetts again enveloped my body. This was my seventh fall season in New England. The vibrant fall foliage display called, "Welcome back to Massachusetts, Jim!" I was more than ready to commence my junior year. At registration, I was handed a note from the Dean of Students' office requesting my presence as soon as possible. Of course I thought the worst as I hurriedly walked to the administration building.

Dean Trent greeted me warmly. He invited me to sit down and proceeded to congratulate me: I had been appointed as a prefect for Morgan Hall, a large men's dormitory. The appointment included free room and board! Additionally, the Board of Trustees had given me a rare scholarship to replace my student loans. I could participate in the work study program, to earn discretionary income.

I couldn't believe my luck. "Thank you so much, Dean Trent!" I said. "You have no idea how much this means."

Dean Trent smiled and said, "You're most welcome, Jim. We want to support our promising students like yourself. We have taken away some of the financial worry for you so that you can concentrate on your studies. Good luck to you this semester and the remainder of the year."

I replied, "I'll study hard and do my best. Please thank the Board of Trustees for their confidence in me!" I literally ran from his office and across campus to Morgan Hall with my single suitcase containing all of my worldly possessions. I checked in and discovered that I was the prefect on the fourth floor. My roommate would be a graduate student. I walked up the stairs to the fourth floor and found my room at the end of the hallway. I opened the door and was pleasantly surprised. The room was large—in fact, it was the largest dorm room I had seen anywhere. It also had its own bathroom and shower!

Brenda spent most of the weekends with me. My roommate was gracious enough to make the room available; most weekends he actually went home, since he lived in a neighboring town. Brenda and I enjoyed the privacy. Our routine was to eat out Friday night, usually at Friendly's. They made a wonderful loaded double cheeseburger and large milkshake, which we shared. Afterward, we usually went to a dance or movie or concert, and then back to my room. The weekends were too short. Sunday evening Brenda returned to Anna Maria. Both of us studied hard during the week in order to maximize our time together during the weekends. There were not many distractions on campus, none of the upheaval we experienced the first two years. It seemed that all students were spending more time studying rather than protesting.

By the fall of 1971, President Nixon's new Vietnam War strategy was well under way. There were less than 160,000 troops remaining in Vietnam. There was talk of ending the war soon. The number of protest marches seemed to decrease; still, President Nixon was not very popular on college campuses across the nation. The peace and antiwar supporters hoped that George McGovern could win the presidency, but President Nixon won re-election by a landslide. He did end the war in Vietnam in 1973. Thousands of war veterans came home and were not treated as war heroes, nor were they respected for their service by most young people and college students. Many Americans thought that we had lost the war—after all, the Communists achieved their objective, one united Vietnam.

The Thanksgiving holiday was upon us. Brenda decided to spend the holiday with her cousin in Hartford, Connecticut. Since I was president of the Black Student Union, I took it upon myself to collect donations of food and clothing for our annual Thanksgiving baskets for the needy. I collected enough food and clothing to distribute to ten needy families. After I delivered the goods, I returned to my dorm and started to fall asleep. My phone began to ring; I thought it was Brenda. I picked up the receiver to speak and to my surprise Dean Trent was on the other end! He said, "Hi Jim. My wife and I thought about you and would like to invite you for Thanksgiving dinner."

I replied, "Oh, yes sir, thank you! That will be much better than Thanksgiving dinner at Friendly's!" We both laughed.

"Very good, Jim," said the dean. "I'll pick you up in

the morning. My family and I look forward to spending Thanksgiving with you."

I awoke early on Thanksgiving so I could get showered and dressed and head downstairs to wait for Dean Trent to arrive. I started to walk out of the front door and saw that we had an overnight snowfall. Somehow I missed the first step, tripped, and fell headfirst into a large snowdrift. The snow was at least a foot deep! I quickly ran back into the dorm to my room to dress in winter gear. I thought to myself, *Mother nature played quite a trick on everyone.* No one expected to see such a large snowfall especially when the weather on the previous day was sunny and temperatures were in the high fifties. I ran back downstairs just in time for Dean Trent to pull up in front of the dorm. We started to laugh about the surprise snowfall. When we arrived at his home, his wife and two sons greeted me warmly. We all watched television, enjoying the Thanksgiving Day parades and all the football games. There seemed to be an endless supply of snacks, and dinner was outstanding. I felt honored to be present with Dean Trent's family.

At day's end, I returned to Morgan Hall for the remainder of the Thanksgiving recess. I was used to the loneliness, as I had spent many Thanksgiving holidays away from home. The Trent family gave me a wonderful basket of food and other goodies, so fortunately I had food to eat. Thank goodness there was a small refrigerator in the room. I talked with Brenda for an hour, and then I decided to eat a small snack and go to bed; after all, nothing was open on campus or in downtown Worcester.

Sunday afternoon arrived none too soon. I was overjoyed to hear noise and movement in the dormitory again. I looked out of my window and saw people everywhere, students accompanied by their parents and friends! Brenda must be back on campus also. I thought to myself, *I'll give her a call.* Brenda had just returned from her cousin's house in Hartford, Connecticut. It seemed that we talked for hours. We both missed each other terribly and we promised each other never to be separated again on holidays.

The remainder of the school semester ended with the start of the Christmas holiday. I had saved enough money to fly home. Granddaddy and Big Mama wanted me to come home and spend some time with my brothers and sisters whom I hadn't seen since the summer. My siblings had grown so much. My brother Victor was seventeen and had assumed the role of eldest child. My sister Janice had become difficult and rebellious. She had become involved with a guy much older whom she ultimately married. My sister Ina was twenty and already married, with a two-year-old daughter, my first niece! Julius, Michael, David, and Linda still lived with Big Mama and Granddaddy. We all enjoyed each other's company, and I realized how much I had missed the wonderful food; after all, no one could cook as well as Big Mama! Early on the morning of Christmas Day we exchanged presents; then I caught the Greyhound to Birmingham to spend the remainder of the holiday with Brenda and her family.

I arrived late Christmas afternoon in Birmingham with a big surprise for Brenda! We both ate dinner with her mom and dad. Near the end of dinner, I presented Brenda with a diamond engagement ring and asked her parents for her hand in marriage. It was a precious moment captured forever in my memory! Brenda and her mom both cried. Her parents gave their permission and blessings. Brenda and I talked and agreed to wait until next year, our senior year, to marry. The entire family started celebrating and did not stop until Brenda and I left to return to college. We discussed our plans for our new life together. There was the possibility of medical school for me, but Brenda would be able to land a teaching job in any state we relocated to. We also decided to delay starting a family. We were so excited about our future!

When Brenda and I returned to our respective colleges to complete our junior year, we agreed to keep a low profile regarding our engagement and marriage plans. We were very focused on academics and our future together. We studied hard and saved the money we earned. I was also busy filing applications to medical schools. During the spring, job fairs on campus popped up, giving students a way to look for employment after graduation. I decided to attend one fair to see what my options were in case I wasn't admitted to medical school. Eastman Kodak was looking for chemists to hire, so I gave them my resume. One week later I received a surprise letter and phone call from Eastman Kodak's recruitment department, offering me a summer internship at their headquarters in Rochester New York. If all went well, I would be given a permanent position as a chemist upon graduation! I was extremely excited and called Brenda at once to share the good news. I wanted her to accompany me to Rochester for the summer. I was surprised by her response; she said, "I can't live with you in Rochester unless we're married." At first, I was stunned since we had agreed to wait to marry at the end of our senior years. But after a moment of silence I answered, "Well then, we're getting married!"

She asked, "When?"

"Before we go to Rochester, silly!"

I could hear the grin on her face when she repeated, "We're getting married!"

The wedding was simple, attended by a few of my classmates and a couple of Brenda's friends. The ceremony was held in the chapel of a small Catholic church near campus, with Father Scanlon officiating. Our honeymoon was one night at the nearby Holiday Inn. Then, it was back to finishing the semester at WPI and Anna Maria College. We were husband and wife! How exciting, how exhilarating! I had the woman I love by my side. Now, I felt whole and complete—ready to conquer the world!

I was due to start my summer internship with Eastman Kodak the second week of June. Brenda and I packed all of our possessions in twenty boxes, loaded it all on a Trailways bus, and headed to Rochester, New York. We arrived without an apartment, but we arranged to stay briefly with a wonderful minister and his wife while we apartment-hunted. This couple was introduced to Brenda and me earlier by one of my classmates at WPI. Their assistance was invaluable as we secured a satisfactory upstairs apartment, completely furnished. The rent was reasonable and the location excellent, within walking distance to the bus stop and stores. Even better, Brenda quickly found a job as a teller at a nearby bank.

My first week at work went well. I was introduced to several staff chemists and assigned as their assistant. Every morning started with a briefing concerning the project we were working on as well as its progress or development. I spent most of my time working with a chemist, Elmer. Elmer and every staff chemist I met had PhDs. I worried that I would need a PhD to have a secure future with any company. Should I forgo working after graduation and obtain my PhD? Should I go to medical school? Well, at least I had the summer to mull things over. For now, I wanted to enjoy my new wife, our marriage, our first apartment together, and being totally independent.

During the first week, Brenda received a phone call from relatives in Buffalo, New York. We were invited to a reception in honor of our recent marriage—after all, we were still newlyweds! At the end of the week we made the short trip to Buffalo by bus. Brenda and I were greeted by several of her cousins and aunts at the bus station, all sisters or cousins of Brenda's mother—the resemblance was striking. They welcomed us immediately; hugs and kisses abounded. We drove to Aunt Carrie's house, where more relatives and friends awaited our arrival. People were gathered outside around an outdoor fire, the smoke from which seemed to keep the mosquitoes at bay. Everyone congratulated us on our recent marriage. Brenda and I were led inside the house to a table displaying a wide range of scrumptious foods: barbecue (chicken and pork), beef, potato salad, candied yams, macaroni and cheese, deviled eggs, collard greens, slaw, hamburgers, hot dogs, smoked sausage, chitlins, and various casseroles. Desserts included pecan pie, coconut and pound cakes, chocolate cake, lemon icebox pie, and more. Since we were the guests of honor, we decided what we wanted and someone served our food to us before anyone else ate. I ate so much that all I could think about was finding somewhere to sleep.

But there was no sleeping allowed at this party! Immediately after eating, everyone moved inside to dance. Brenda and I passed on dancing initially, preferring to be spectators. What a sight it was! One family friend, who was quite inebriated, including lots of pelvic thrusting and other sexually explicit moves in her dancing, which we found highly entertaining. Several men tried to dance with her, but no one could match her energy. The evening ended late, around 2:30 a.m. Brenda and I slept most of the next day, but by early afternoon we were ready for the trip back to Rochester.

Monday morning came early. That week, several upper-level executives attended the morning briefing. What I heard was intriguing. Eastman Kodak, a major producer of film for cameras for photography and medical imaging, was searching for a replacement for silver. Silver is a key component in the film base emulsion, necessary for permanently capturing or recording an image or picture. The chemists of Eastman Kodak were asked to develop a cheaper alternative. Elmer and the other chemists began working on this project immediately. Various alternatives to silver were investigated and tested. The most promising alternatives were a class of organic pigments. My primary role as an assistant was to carry out actual experiments that created these new compounds for prototype testing. I also participated in many of the research team meetings held to design these compounds. This was exciting stuff! I was helping invent something new, which had the potential to help Eastman Kodak! My boyhood dream to contribute to the advancement of science and humanity was starting to be realized. Every morning upon waking up, I was thankful for and thrilled to be involved in such an endeavor.

Following a particularly successful week of research and of testing a promising discovery, Elmer and I were rewarded with a free dinner by the research team. Elmer also decided to treat me to an afternoon of sailing. He was a sailing enthusiast, and he spent a great deal of his recreational time sailing his catamaran on the Finger Lakes in the Rochester area. The afternoon we went sailing was perfect. The weather was magnificent:, brilliant sunshine, a mild, steady breeze with temperatures in the seventies. We sailed for about ninety minutes and talked about a variety of subjects. He asked me if I would consider coming to work full time after graduation. I was honored and stated that I would strongly consider the offer after discussing the matter with my wife. Suddenly, a strong breeze filled the catamaran sails and the boat started to tilt! I panicked! Was I going to drown? Elmer laughed and reassured me that everything was under control. He asked me to assist him by balancing the catamaran while he managed the sails. He instructed me to lean over the boat backwards. It worked! Elmer regained control of the boat. We decided to call it a day and returned to shore. I decided then and there never to accept another sailing invitation!

As summer drew to a close, Brenda and I were invited to a meeting with Eastman Kodak executives to formally discuss the offer for employment. The offer was most appealing. I was offered $16,000 annually to start as a first-year chemist. Additionally, I was offered an executive track, which would lead to securing an MBA. They would cover my educational expenses. Bonuses were also possible at the end of every year. Brenda and I looked at each other in disbelief; it all sounded too good to be true! We were allowed to talk in private for fifteen minutes, after which I accepted the offer pending the results of medical school applications. If I got into medical school, obviously I would go to medical school. Privately, Brenda was irritated that I would give up such a promising offer to attend medical school. Medical school and specialty training would delay earning any substantial income for at least eight years! I reassured her that I understood the financial sacrifice but felt that I would be happier with life as a doctor.

Back at school, I was extremely busy. Again, I was appointed as a prefect for a coeducational dorm floor located in Riley Hall. I had the additional responsibilities of trustee meetings and Black Student Union duties. I was busy completing and sending applications to medical schools, and I had to arrange to take the MCAT examination, one of the requirements for medical school applicants. Also, I needed to arrange travel for medical school interviews. As a senior chemistry major, I was required to design and complete a year-long research project as well as a thesis. My entire senior chemistry grade was based upon the successful completion of this project and thesis. Brenda and I treasured our time together, even though we only managed to see each other on the weekends. She was my refuge and I hers. I knew that she was my soul mate. We both were young, gifted, and black; devoted to each other, nonviolence, tolerance, and creating a better America for our children as well as others. I felt that we were like-minded in all of our goals and beliefs. We both were aware of the obstacles and challenges that lay ahead, particularly if we wanted to return to the South, and we did want to.

I spent three weeks designing my senior chemistry research project. My faculty advisor helped with valuable suggestions. Professor Dulos was young, energetic, and bright. His thesis research involved work with porphyrins, a unique class of compounds similar to human hemoglobin. I reasoned that I could design an *in vitro* experiment using these compounds to simulate human hemoglobin. I was interested in a disease that mostly African Americans suffered from: sickle cell anemia. This was a hereditary disease affecting the shape of red blood cells. Anything that reduces the amount of oxygen available to the red blood cells will cause the cells to distort, and the shape looked like a sickle (hence the name). Numerous small blood vessels are partially or completely blocked by these distorted red blood cells. The individual experiences intense pain. There is the risk of serious damage to any of the internal organs of the body. The sickle process may also cause the individual to die. In 1972, most sickle cell anemia patients died early, most succumbing by age forty. The goal of my research was to identify compounds and chemicals that change the environment surrounding red blood cells, in order to prevent or reverse the sickle process. I hoped that this type of research would ultimately lead to identifying non-toxic drugs to effectively treat this disease. My research would involve performing a vast number of mathematical calculations. Using a slide rule to manually perform all the necessary calculations would be impossible. However, WPI was the recent recipient of a large computer that completely filled the basement floor of Goddard Hall. One used a terminal to access the computer. Remember, this was when computer programs were produced by punch cards: a single program could easily fill a large box!

I also continued preparing for medical school. I arranged to take the MCAT exam at Harvard University in October. I met several Harvard undergraduates who were taking the MCAT exam, and I was encouraged to apply to Harvard Medical School, which I did. Yet, deep down inside of me I wanted to return to Tennessee for medical school. The MCAT results were available in six weeks. I arranged for interviews to begin in the late fall. My itinerary included visits to University of Massachusetts School of Medicine, University of Tennessee at Memphis, St. Louis University School of Medicine, and Washington University School of Medicine. My trip would start in Worcester and end in St. Louis, Missouri, with a layover stop in Memphis. My visits went very well. I was told that I was accepted to St. Louis University and Washington University at the end of each of those interviews! During my stop in Memphis, I met with the dean of the School of Medicine at the airport, who told me I had been accepted at the University of Tennessee! I also received an admissions letter to attend the University Massachusetts after I had returned to Worcester.

Brenda and I discussed the offers at length. Of course, I was a resident of the state of Tennessee, so my tuition at the University of Tennessee would be much lower than the tuitions of the other medical schools I applied to—$1600 per year as opposed to near $20,000 a year. The School of Medicine offered a three-year program rather than a four-year program, too, which meant I could move on to practice sooner. Additionally, the University of Tennessee promised full tuition support. Memphis was within easy driving distance of both Brenda's home and mine. Brenda also discovered that there was a need in Memphis for special education, her teaching specialty. Moreover, she also had a cousin living in Memphis, which meant it wouldn't feel so lonely. So, Memphis and University of Tennessee it was!

I informed Eastman Kodak of my decision to attend medical school rather than accept their employment offer. Some of my family members questioned my decision to turn down a good-paying position in favor of more school. I even had some fear about my decision. By the end of medical school, internship and residency, and specialty training, I would have loans to repay and be far behind my contemporaries in earnings. What if something went wrong such that I could not complete medical school? What would or could I do? However, these were uncertainties and odds I was willing to face to reach a dream that began when I was a young boy. Yes, I was going to medical school to become a doctor!

The first semester of my senior year ended successfully. Brenda and I were doing well academically. I scored well on the MCAT examination and also made the honor roll. We both headed to Birmingham for our first Christmas together as husband and wife. We were given a delayed wedding reception. I think I became addicted to my mother-in-law's sweet potato pie, often devouring a whole pie in one day!

On Christmas Day afternoon Brenda and I headed to Chattanooga to spend part of the Christmas holiday with Big Mama, Granddaddy, and my brothers and sisters. We exchanged gifts, and shared our experiences of the past six months. There was no shortage of vintage Big Mama cuisine, so, so good and so, so delicious! Brenda and I returned to Birmingham to spend New Year's Eve and New Year's Day, and then it was time to head back to college to finish and graduate.

Because I had already gotten into med school, I was able to devote my undivided attention to completing my chemistry thesis and research project; Brenda started the application process to secure a teaching position in Memphis. I spent long hours writing computer programs to perform the innumerable mathematical calculations required. By spring, I had collected enough data to support my theory and proceeded to write my thesis. I also constructed a computerized model to demonstrate my theory and my results. I had finished everything and submitted my work to my advisor and chemistry professor, Professor Dulos, before Mother's Day in early May. I was called to his office several days later to hear his critique of my thesis and project, and to find out what my final grade would be. Professor Dulos was highly impressed with my work. In fact, he graded the entire project as excellent, and awarded me an A for the entire year! He also informed me that he found my project good enough to enter it in the American Chemical Society, Massachusetts Chapter, awards competition, which would take place in two weeks. I was invited to present my project, and I won first prize, a cash reward of $50! The publicity was good for WPI to have an undergraduate win such an award, and of course it was good for me to receive the recognition!

At last, I graduated. The president of the university handed me my diploma, shook my hand, and offered to announce that I would be attending medical school. I replied, "No sir, I will go quietly, like I came." I stuck by my mantra, to be a force for quiet change. Now, it was on to Memphis.

CHAPTER 4

Medical School and Internship

The elation and giddiness of being a college graduate, a first for my family, soon passed. The reality of the daunting task ahead was sobering. The University of Tennessee graduated doctors in three years to help alleviate a severe doctor shortage in Tennessee. The core curriculum was the same as four-year programs but without as many electives. Additionally, there was no traditional summer break. The curriculum was continuous for thirty-six straight months with two week breaks between ten- or twelve-week quarters. I graduated from college on June 2; medical school was scheduled to start July 1! There was not enough time for Brenda to find a job, although she scheduled several interviews once we got to Memphis. I fretted somewhat over details like housing, furniture, transportation, and so on. However, I fell into a puddle of good luck. Ten days prior to the start of medical school, Brenda informed me that her dad was giving us a loan to buy furniture; we got confirmation for a one-bedroom apartment located within a newly constructed apartment complex located within ten minutes' walking distance to the medical school, and Brenda received a job offer from Memphis city schools prior to any interviews! As a gift, her dad purchased a used 1965 Mustang to use as a down payment for the purchase of a new car. When I selected our furniture for the apartment, her dad paid for it, but I considered it a loan and promised to repay it. Brenda's brother Eddie volunteered to help us with the move to Memphis and I gratefully accepted this help.

I did not sleep well the night before the move. I had been sleeping poorly since graduation worrying about my decision to go to medical school. I wondered if I should have stayed in Massachusetts, or gone to St. Louis. The first rays of dawn were starting to creep above the horizon; I was wide awake and it was the morning of the move to Memphis. We loaded up the U-Haul, the Mustang in tow, and started the drive to Memphis.

We drove northwest on Highway 78, passing through the rolling hills and small towns of Alabama and Mississippi. Millions of thoughts raced through my mind. Superficially, to many upwardly-mobile educated and energetic young African Americans, the notion of returning to the old South was professional suicide. The voices of many of my contemporaries, advisors, family members, and friends reverberated in my head: *Jim, you are facing long odds, an uphill battle. You think just because you are educated, you will be accepted and successful. Remember, you are in the South, where the law is hatred—hate your neighbors if they are black, go to church on Sunday, and forget.*

Memphis, the city that refused to practice brotherly love. Memphis, the city that assassinated Martin Luther King. Memphis, located near the home of General Nathan Bedford, founder of the Ku Klux Klan. Yet, I came with high hopes of contributing to the growth of the new South out of the old, which was created on the back of my ancestors, the soil stained with their blood, sweat, and tears. This was hallowed ground. I felt honored to stand on it. Yes, thousands of educated blacks were returning as the vanguard of a new beginning, the start of building a new legacy for our children and others who followed.

Nearly seven hours passed before we reached Memphis. The blazing afternoon sun and humid air made the temperature seem hotter than the ninety-four degree temperature displayed on a billboard we passed. The apartment complex where we would reside was easily reached. Methodically, Brenda, Eddie, and I unloaded our cargo, transporting it to our apartment on the third floor. Fortunately, a freight elevator was available for use. Our apartment had a balcony that offered a near panoramic view of the downtown skyline, which looked impressive to me. The tallest building sported a large UP (Union Planters Bank) emblem and was over forty stories tall. The other tall buildings present ranged from twenty to thirty stories tall. Turning east, the sprawling medical complex, which included the medical school, could be seen; Baptist Hospital dominated the skyline. A slight breeze crossed my face. I started to relax and thought to myself, *There is a lot of potential here.* Memphis could become another Atlanta, a bustling, vibrant metropolis in the South. I had the feeling that if there were any other like-minded young professionals here, then Memphis would be on the verge of becoming a top-tier city.

Suddenly, Brenda's voice snapped me out of my daydreaming. "Jimmy,"—she always called me that—"come on, honey, let's finish unpacking. Eddie has to go back to Birmingham tomorrow morning."

I replied, "Okay, honey. I was just daydreaming about Memphis. I'm starting to feel really good about this place."

Once we finished unpacking and placing furniture, it was after eight. We grabbed a quick bite, and it was not long before we were all stretching and yawning. The next morning after breakfast, Eddie left to return to Birmingham in the U-Haul. Brenda and I thanked him profusely for his help. That night, we went to bed early; medical school would start for me in the morning.

It was Thursday morning, the first day of medical school.

I got up early, said goodbye to Brenda, and walked briskly to the medical school campus. The student activities building was crowded with registering students. There was a sea of young eager faces; future doctors, nurses, pharmacists, and lab technicians signed registration papers before heading downstairs to the campus bookstore. Two hours later, I had completed this process and headed back to the apartment with books and supplies. I eagerly displayed by traditional doctor's bag that contained my tuning fork, stethoscope, reflex hammer, and blood pressure apparatus. Brenda decided to let me take her blood pressure and became my first patient. We planned to relax the remainder of the day. Tomorrow, medical student orientation began, as well as the first day of classes, and Brenda was scheduled to begin work the following Monday.

The Mustang needed lots of repair work, and Brenda needed reliable transportation, so we decided to visit car dealerships later that afternoon. We barely made it to the first dealership in the Mustang. In fact, I was sure that it had traveled its last mile. We needed a new vehicle or we might have to walk home! We were at a Chevrolet dealership and quickly chose a new compact car, a Chevy Vega. The entire purchase process went quickly; we had no trouble qualifying for a car loan as Brenda had her signed contract in hand. We drove back to the apartment in our new car! As we were about to park, the thought occurred to me that Brenda really didn't know how to drive. She had barely passed her exam. I decided to give her some quick lessons by letting her drive around the parking lot. I was confident that she would learn quickly. I moved over to the passenger seat, she to the driver's seat. The first time we drove around the parking lot, she barely missed hitting a light pole! She got better as we continued to practice for about thirty minutes. We parked the car and headed to the apartment, ate dinner, watched television, and then went to bed. That night I had a couple of nightmares about Brenda's driving!

Friday morning was the first day of scheduled classes. There were approximately 105 to 110 medical students in my first-year class. We all gathered in the student auditorium to hear and meet the medical school administration, deans, and faculty. It was at this meeting that I discovered a total of five black students in my first-year class. The University of Tennessee by tradition seemed unable to recruit and retain qualified African American medical students. The perception was a mixture of bias or racism, of insensitivity to the needs of the students such as financial support, mentoring, and tutoring. Often, African American applicants accepted for admission would elect to go elsewhere. A short meeting occurred after the main orientation, involving key members of the administration and the five of us. We were all reassured of the medical school's commitment to our success. Mr. Roland Wood, the only African American administrator, was introduced to us as a contact person who would monitor our progress, address our concerns, and arrange for tutoring when necessary. It was very comforting to all of us that we had an intermediary and hopefully a friend to help us along this three-year journey to obtain medical degrees.

One of the students, David, lived near my apartment. He and his wife Sharon invited Brenda and me over to their apartment to socialize after classes ended. We absolutely had a ball! This was the beginning of a long friendship. Brenda and Sharon were both school teachers and bonded right away. We socialized together on as many Friday nights as the grueling medical school schedule allowed.

Monday morning came too soon. I watched as Brenda drove off to begin her first day of teaching. I was proud that she had learned to drive so well so quickly. The practice sessions I had with her following the first scary practice were rather tame. I left, and arrived to my first class on time. This was the dreaded anatomy course. The professor was a diminutive woman with flaming red hair named Joan Harris. Following her introductory remarks, we were led to the laboratory to meet our human cadavers, our companions for the next six months. Most of the cadavers were elderly individuals who had donated their bodies to the medical school to help teach human anatomy. I was assigned to a cadaver I named Lucy. Her peaceful facial expression helped me to relax a bit. Lucy and the other cadavers had the strong smell of formaldehyde, overpowering at first but less of a distraction as the course progressed. Everyone could tell that we were first-year students; we all had that unmistakable formaldehyde smell on our hands, in our hair, and on our clothes. Even our books, especially the anatomy book, possessed that unmistakable formaldehyde smell. Brenda hated sleeping with me because of it; I spent many nights on the couch during the six months of the anatomy course. Some of those nights I dreamed of Lucy and wondered about her family and about her origins. I wondered why she decided to donate her body to science. I was thankful for such unselfish individuals who helped contribute to my medical education. Later during my radiology residency training, I realized how important Lucy and that anatomy course had been.

Biochemistry was another first-year course that included a required laboratory. Because of my chemistry major in college, the biochemistry professor excused me from the laboratory requirement. Instead, I was assigned to a special research project. My biochemistry professor somehow knew about my chemistry research project and the award I had won. I was introduced to Professor Laurin, who was well-known nationally as a leader in sickle-cell research. I got the extreme honor and privilege of working with Professor Laurin on developing chemical compounds that could reverse the sickling process. We performed animal studies to evaluate the side effects and toxicity of the chemical compounds we developed. The chemical compounds deemed safe for human use got used in clinical trials. One of the most promising compounds developed was a phosphate compound. Other compounds were developed, but my six-month assignment to the research laboratory ended prior to the conclusion of testing. I was thrilled and fulfilled because of this experience. I had experienced a portion of my dream: to use my scientific background to benefit mankind.

The end of the Christmas holiday marked the beginning of the second semester. The message board in the student activities center had a note for me from the associate dean. I immediately thought the worst. Grades had not yet been posted. Was I in academic trouble? The meeting with the dean was not about my academic performance—in fact, he told me that I had done well. I did not want to hear the other news or information he gave me, which was about financial support. The grant monies that I thought were available had vanished. The dean immediately started discussing my options, including loans, work, or taking off six months to secure other financing. I was stunned, but I thanked him for his help. I made it home to the apartment, and Brenda immediately spotted a negative look on my face. "What's wrong, Jimmy?"

I replied, "There's no money for me to finish the first year! The grant funding that I thought was secure wasn't. I don't know what to do. We don't have the money, our families don't, banks won't give us a loan. What are we going to do?"

She shook her head. "We can't give up, Jimmy! Have faith that we will find something!" She was right. I needed to remain focused and find funding soon. Serendipitously, the answer appeared in the morning newspaper in an ad for the Armed Forces of the United States. The Navy, Air Force, and Army had a severe shortage of doctors. They were aggressively recruiting future doctors in medical school by offering to pay all medical school expenses, including the purchase of books and supplies with a stipend of $400 a month. Additionally, the successful applicant would become a commissioned officer and would receive the full pay associated with his or her rank during the six weeks of the year assigned to active duty. The active-duty assignment would be to continue medical school uninterrupted! In return, upon graduation from medical school, one would serve as a doctor in the military, one year for each year of financial support received during medical school. Since the University of Tennessee medical school was three years, my military obligation would be three years upon finishing medical school.

The military option was just what I needed; my medical school financial worries were over! I too would serve my country like my dad and brother Victor, who was in the ROTC program. I chose to apply to the United States Navy Medical Corps because of the strength and reputation of their medical department. The navy reviewed my application and invited me to complete a physical examination, a requirement for military service. I traveled to Chelsea, Massachusetts, for an extensive physical, which I passed! I was also asked if I was interested in becoming a flight surgeon because of my exceptional visual acuity. I was flattered but refused this offer. Approximately two weeks later, I received a large package welcoming me; I had been accepted to receive the scholarship money to finance the remainder of medical school! I was surprised to discover that many of my classmates had also applied for this military program and were also accepted. It was odd to me in some respects. I had become a part of the military I had protested against while in college.

One thing medical students must quickly acclimate to is the frequency of testing and the massive amounts of information one had to assimilate to successfully pass tests. The students who were not successful flunked out or dropped out. One student committed suicide. I, like other classmates, could not understand why someone would take his or her own life. It was puzzling and rocked us to the core. I recalled that a student had committed suicide at WPI during my senior year, in the dorm where I was a prefect. At that time, I was shocked by the incident and buried my feelings about it. In an instant my thoughts returned to the matter at hand: exam time. Everyone seemed to be associated with study groups except for us, the African American students. We decided to study together and soon discovered that we were disadvantaged by not having access to test research or previous exams given by our professors, which came with answers as well as commentary and references. This material was an invaluable study aid because it gave one a sense of the information professors really wanted you to know. Medical students associated with fraternities were usually the only ones with access to this valuable information. As a result, they collectively scored better on all exams, usually 15 percent higher than non-fraternity students. Our class decided to obtain this information and was successful in retrieving it after the first series of exams.

We realized that our ultimate success would be to reach out and cultivate relationships with the other members of our class. Henceforth, study groups were no longer segregated. The bonds of friendship with others formed during this time would last well past graduation. We all shared the same goal of becoming the best doctors possible, so we all studied together and shared the test research. This collaborative study effort made us all more tolerant of differences and contributed to our personal growth as human beings.

The neuroanatomy course, taught by Dr. Bruce, was every medical student's favorite. Dr. Bruce's demeanor was that of a kind, compassionate father figure, highly respected by all. He was one of the few professors I met at this level of the educational process who displayed a passion for teaching young, future doctors. Today, I consider him to be another one of the influential educators who made a difference in my life. The enthusiasm he generated within me made the rest of the second part of my first year seem easy. It was exam time again as the first year ended. Again, group study and test research benefited all, and we all passed.

Following a short summer break, the second year began. This would be the last six months of classroom teaching. Our class had developed into a well-oiled studying machine. We all agreed to study individually, then meet for group study and go over test research. This strategy continued to work well. However, this type of dedication to study and master vast amounts of information consumed large blocks of time—time away from husbands or wives and children, which obviously strained personal relationships. Several couples separated, some divorced. Little did we all realize that these events were harbingers of the days ahead.

The first six months of the second year ended as quickly as they began. The second half of the year was the beginning of the clinical part of our education, the beginning of hands-on patient contact, the essence of the doctor-patient relationship. My colleagues and I quickly realized that our knowledge base was only an introduction to the world of medicine. Each passing day of our clinical experience reminded us how little we really knew. The staff doctors, residents, interns, and nurses constantly reminded us of the paucity of our knowledge. The teaching style at this level of medical education was to embarrass and shame the students in public, in front of an audience. The idea was to keep us highly motivated to read and study constantly to avoid embarrassment. It worked. Massive amounts of data regarding patient care had to be assimilated quickly. Still, actual involvement with patient care was the best teacher of all. Seeing and touching patients and successfully treating their diseases was far more memorable and instructive than memorizing facts from a book.

The largest adjustment for my colleagues and me was getting used to the long hours spent away from home and in the hospital. Patient care had no clock, no real beginning or end. The concept of night call was foreign not only to us medical students but also to our families. Those of us who made it through the first half of medical school and were ignorant of the demanding and grueling hours required for patient care were stunned. The thought of 24/7 care, that you the doctor are responsible and on call for your patient twenty-four hours a day, seemed overwhelming to me, Brenda, my peers, and their spouses. This fact, this reality cast a shadow over our relationships with our spouses. Brenda's response (like that of many other spouses) was very negative. She thought I was lying about the many hours of night call I had to endure, not only for medical school, but also for the rest of my professional life.

My typical day for the clinical part of medical school began at 6:30 a.m. It was expected that history and physical exams of newly admitted patients after 5 p.m. would be completed by the time morning rounds started by the assigned medical student, who would have it and any lab results ready for the intern. The intern reported to the resident, who reported to the assigned staff doctor, who was usually part of the university faculty or was a private practice doctor with an academic appointment. The staff doctor usually arrived around 8 a.m. The entourage of doctors in training all reported and discussed diagnosis and treatment plans for all newly admitted patients. This discussion took place in a formal setting in the auditorium or a large conference room. Following this meeting, each team of medical students, interns, residents, and staff doctors conducted rounds on their assigned patients. The medical treatment of each patient and their response to therapy was analyzed and discussed, as were plans for therapy, change of therapeutic regimens, and anticipated discharge dates.

For me, it was amazing to witness how well the interns and residents knew their patients and how well the patients were cared for considering that these individuals had been on call, completing a thirty-six-hour day with less than two hours of sleep. Most interns practically lived in the hospital, spending in excess of 120 hours per week there. It was not uncommon for an intern to spend most of the night at the bedside of a very ill patient. There were no kudos or pats on the back; it was expected. As medical students, we all aspired to reach that level of professional competence and physical durability. Nothing less than perfection was tolerated, so a perfectionist I became. For the rest of my adult life, I pursued perfection and perfection consumed me; in my mind it *became* me. Nothing else mattered; even family was sacrificed. I rationalized that once my training was over, I could enjoy the fruits of my labor with my family. Unfortunately, I and many of my colleagues discovered later in life that there were painful consequences, including loss of family from divorce, premature death, and personal issues, some leading to mental issues, some leading to addiction issues. Even perfection wasn't worth it.

Near the end of the second year, several more of my classmates had separated or divorced spouses.

The summer of 1975 ushered in the third and last year of medical school. Those of us who had made it to this point sensed an air of acceptance, newly baptized in the waters of clinical medicine. I noticed a new confidence within me. My shy, soft nature was being replaced by a resolute firmness, an erect posture, a projecting voice, a new swagger. My patient responsibility increased. One of my rotations included being assigned as the acting intern in the old West Tennessee Chest Hospital. In other words, I was the intern. I was responsible for the care of all patients on my assigned floor, approximately fifteen to twenty patients. Patient rounds were performed with the residents and staff doctor only. Once finished, I was left alone to managed and care for my assigned patients, a sort of baptism by fire. The long hours and independence built confidence. I knew all of my patients' names and histories as well as their clinical course and estimated discharge date, usually without referring to my trusty note cards (I made reference cards containing each patient's vital information). Once a particular patient was discharged, I retired his note card to my professional files at home. Many of my colleagues often referred to these cards as their peripheral brain. We used the cards placed in storage as teaching aids for future patient care.

Somehow, I managed to find a balance between being a

busy medical student and a husband. Brenda and I, like any other couple, struggled with the demands of her job and my busy schedule. We both tried to make Friday night a time of relaxation, a time for each other, and a time for friends. One of our favorite gathering spots was Overton Square's TGI Fridays. We were fortunate and thankful to have discretionary income for occasional dining out, movies, and concerts. We decided that we could afford a larger place too. Our current apartment was less than six hundred square feet, but there were newly constructed apartments in the Raleigh area that were affordable and bigger. Several of my classmates decided to move into the two-bedroom townhouse apartments.

On moving day, I discovered that we did not get the townhouse apartment we wanted, and were assigned an apartment on the second floor. There were no elevators! Thank goodness for the moving company guys who readily assisted us transporting furniture to our second-floor apartment. Brenda and I were dead tired by the end of the day. It was quiet, the night was calm, moonlight streamed into our bedroom window. We fell fast asleep in each other's arms.

The commute for Brenda to work and for me to the medical center was approximately equal, fifteen minutes. We both were pleased with the move and content in our new apartment. It was quiet and peaceful for approximately one month when we did not have a next-door neighbor. I could read and study without any noise. This tranquility abruptly ended with the arrival of a next-door neighbor. It continued to be quiet during the day, but the exact opposite occurred at sunset, with the loud thumping sound of Barry White's music accompanied by the intense smell of marijuana. The noise usually ended by midnight during the week, but lasted all night on the weekends. I decided not to tolerate the annoyance any further. One evening I walked next door to my neighbor's apartment, knocked on the door, and came face-to-face with them for the first time. I explained that I was a medical student and that my wife worked and that we both needed to sleep at night. They both appeared highly intoxicated but were cordial and agreed to be quieter neighbors at night. However, the next night it was business as usual! In fact, the music seemed to be louder than ever, the marijuana smell more intense! I was pissed! I complained to the apartment manager who in turn gave a verbal warning to the offending couple. The situation continued to deteriorate, however. Brenda and I were not the only couple complaining about our neighbors, but it seemed that their anger was directed at Brenda and me.

Several days passed. I arrived home early one afternoon after finishing hospital duties and immediately saw that my apartment door was ajar! I raced up the stairs to the apartment, completely opened the front door and gasped at what I saw. Most of our furniture and clothing was gone. The television, stereo, and all records were gone. I slowly sank to the living room floor, eyes watering, anger growing, bewildered and in disbelief that someone would dare to violate our privacy and steal our stuff! Of course I had a hunch who the culprit was. I walked out of my apartment to the apartment next door and confirmed my hunch: the neighbors were gone, the apartment empty! They had burglarized my apartment, stolen our stuff, and moved! Later, I found out that actually they had been evicted. This was retaliation, Memphis-style. One of the reasons I chose to come to Memphis was that I felt it would have less crime than a large metropolitan area like St. Louis. I recall the medical students I talked with at Washington University warning me of the high crime rate in St. Louis. Still I was naïve. I learned a valuable lesson about safety, always installing deadbolt locks thereafter. My renter's insurance alleviated some of the financial loss, but I was highly disappointed by the act of thievery and invasion of privacy. This episode hurt deeply and was the beginning of the type of welcome this native son of Tennessee would continue to receive.

I buried the incident within my subconscious and continued with the business at hand: finishing medical school. I was thankful that there was no bodily harm to Brenda or me. Finally, the townhouse apartment became available within days of this incident, so we moved. Our brief period of feeling secure was again shattered when, several weeks after moving, we were again burglarized, losing the television and stereo equipment. Thereafter, I purchased a handgun and installed a cheap alarm system. We did not experience another burglary.

The arrival of 1976 bought with it the hope and the promise of better days ahead. The turbulent '60s, peace marches, homegrown terrorism, Vietnam War, recession of 1973–74, and Arab oil embargo were all being relegated to the pages of history books. The passionate feelings and discussions regarding politics and social issues seemed to wane. It was as if everyone were just plain tired of confrontation and fighting. America's core beliefs of honesty, decency, and fair play had been desecrated by the Watergate scandal and a president who thought he was above the law. President Nixon resigned rather than face impeachment in 1974. Many of his advisers and aides faced criminal charges and jail time for their roles in the Watergate scandal and its cover-up. America needed new leadership not corrupted by Washington politics. 1976 was an election year, a chance to correct the wrongs of the previous Republican administration. It was with this enthusiasm for change that I launched myself into the last half of my final year of school. This was the Bicentennial celebration of the birth of America. I wanted to be able to say to our founding fathers with a clear conscience, "See, we got it right!"

The last six months of medical school went smoothly for me. My patient responsibility increased, and I was assigned to more night call. Night call ended at 11 p.m., and I reassured Brenda that it was better than being there all night. The poor intern would have been up all night when I saw him or her the next morning. I dreaded the thought of my internship and the night call that would start for me in July.

I did get to experience a night call that lasted all night before graduating from medical school, and of course it happened at the most inopportune time. I was assigned a night call the day before extremely important clinical examinations consisting of the oral presentation of an assigned topic. The presentation would be a thorough discussion of a disease, including its pathophysiology and treatment. These presentations were expected to be thorough and were expected to last about forty-five minutes. The evening of my night call, the intern and I admitted a seriously ill patient. The shift ended for me as usual, and I expected to leave to finalize my oral presentation examination for the next day. The seriously ill patient had been stabilized, so I went to check out with my intern. To my surprise, the intern strongly suggested that I stay to help him. I informed him that the oral presentation examination grade represented the entire grade for the medical rotation I was assigned to. Still, he insisted that he needed my help, so I stayed.

I was up all night gathering lab and other data, checking on patients, and answering calls for assistance from nurses, functions that the intern was assigned to do. I noticed that the intern had disappeared for several hours. I finally found him reading and preparing for rounds in the morning. I felt like I had been had. Later that night some of the nurses informed me that my other medical student colleagues had been released early, around 9 p.m., to prepare for their clinical presentation exams. The nurses thought that I was being taken advantage of, and I was furious!

I arrived home the next morning at 7:30 a.m., completely exhausted. I was hungry, unshaven, and sweaty. My clinical oral presentation examination was scheduled to start promptly at 8:30 a.m. I pleaded with the professor conducting the oral examinations for a one-day reprieve since I had been up all night involved with patient care. He refused my request, stating that I was supposed to go home at 9 p.m. like my other colleagues. He did not want to listen to any of my explanations, and he demanded that I start my presentation as scheduled. "Tell me everything you know about acute renal disease its causes, pathophysiology, and treatment. You must be very thorough!"

I was so tired that my vision was blurred; however, my adrenaline kicked in, and I began my oral presentation. I thought the dissertation was going well. I ended with one minute to spare. Dr. Ackerman, the examining professor, started his critique. "Most of your discussion was adequate; however, you did not give me the exact detailed information I requested, especially regarding pathophysiology! You appear tired and ungroomed—what is your excuse?" When I reminded him, he barked, "I don't care if you've been up all night!" He did not speak another word and glared at me coldly and arrogantly. Then, he dismissed me curtly, saying, "You may go, Dr. Ellis!"

I left thinking I'd lost the A I was expecting. I was late for rounds at the VA hospital, so I quickened my pace, battling hunger, anger, and sleep deprivation. I did not know how to process my feelings. I wondered how another human being could so thoroughly dehumanize another in the name of teaching! Was this initiation to this noble profession a rite of passage, or was it, as it appeared to me, just plain sadistic? In order to move on, I buried these feelings deep within my subconscious.

I had to make several important decisions during this last six months of medical school. I had to decide where I would do my internship and what my residency specialty training should be. I received a letter from the United States Navy Medical Corps just before I applied for internships. The Medical Corps wanted me to do my internship in the Navy. My choices were primarily the Naval Regional Medical Centers located in Portsmouth, Virginia, San Diego, California, and Bethesda, Maryland. I chose the Naval Hospital in Portsmouth, Virginia. Additionally, the Medical Corps wanted me to declare a specialty for residency training and to choose one of the residency training programs offered by the Navy. One of the disadvantages of the three-year medical program was the lack of elective time, which was usually spent in several of the specialties. My medical school curriculum allowed for only two electives. I had studied radiology and obstetrics.

The obstetrics rotation was located within the regional medical center's labor and delivery area. Most of the patients were indigent and usually presented to labor and delivery in labor, without any prior prenatal care. I enjoy the thrill of delivering live healthy babies and presenting these babies to their mothers. The mom, usually no older than seventeen, was always thankful for the medical care she and her baby received. Some of the babies delivered were premature, and received excellent neonatal care in one of the best neonatal intensive care units in the nation.

The radiology rotation was also a thrill for me. I believed that radiology was an invaluable asset to patient care. Most medical students had a rather negative view of the importance of the specialty, considering it too detached from direct patient care. They believed radiologists tended to be lazy, were poor communicators, and spent most of their day sitting on their butts and drinking coffee.

By contrast, I discovered that radiologists performed and interpreted many difficult medical tests, such as angiograms, myelograms, bronchograms, arthrograms, percutaneous biopsies, pneumoencephalograms, fluoroscopy, barium studies, and tomograms. The radiologists had to have a very broad knowledge base of normal and pathologic anatomy in order to accurately interpret the radiographs produced from the many radiology procedures. New radiology machines were being developed that would be able to look inside the human body and produce images of anatomy and pathologic processes noninvasively. In 1976, radiologists also performed radiation therapy for cancer patients.

The radiology department chairman at the University of Tennessee College of Medicine, Jack Rubinsky, was legendary, conducting conferences and mesmerizing the audience with his superior diagnostic acumen and accuracy. Every Friday afternoon, radiology residents challenged the radiology staff to interpret the most difficult cases they could gather, with the goal of finding cases that the staff doctors could not diagnose. Usually, most of the staff would not participate to avoid being embarrassed. Friday became the Rubinsky show. He accepted all challenges from the residents and, amazingly, could interpret and diagnose every unknown case presented to him! In retrospect, if I had been asked who or what was the most influential regarding my decision to consider radiology as a specialty, I would have to say Dr. Jack Rubinsky.

Although it was difficult for me to decide on a specialty, I knew I thoroughly enjoyed one of the happiest moments in medicine, the birth of a child, and so I chose to specialize in obstetrics. Despite that, years later, I regretted shortening my medical school experience by selecting a three-year program. (The University of Tennessee College of Medicine eventually ended the three-year program, returning to a four-year program.)

I knew I was going to Portsmouth, Virginia, for my internship. Since I had chosen obstetrics and gynecology as my residency, the Medical Corps informed me that the obstetrics program was a four-year training program, and that the first year of residency would be my internship year. This meant that I would spend the entire internship year in the obstetrics and gynecology program. I could remain at the Naval Hospital and finish all of my postgraduate training. One fact I had missed was that none of my postgraduate training counted toward the reduction of my obligated service to the United States Medical Corps, which was three years. Therefore, I would spend seven years in the Navy Medical Corps! *Oh well,* I thought, *I can't change anything now.* Besides, my internship and residency pay would exceed what my peers earned. I was content.

Winter turned into spring and my thoughts were consumed by my approaching graduation. Events seemed to speed up, and graduation day arrived before I knew it. I was jubilant! Brenda, my sister Janice, and Janice's husband attended the graduation ceremony, held in the Mid-South Coliseum. With immense pride, I accepted the challenge of the Hippocratic oath, then received my diploma. *James Van Norwood Ellis, Doctor of Medicine, June 5, 1976.* I was officially a doctor! We five African Americans were the largest number of African American doctors produced by the University of Tennessee College of Medicine to date. There were celebrations and hugs; no one, not ever, could take away this accomplishment!

There was not much time to celebrate and revel in our accomplishment, however; internships began promptly on July 1. Brenda and I needed to secure an apartment in Portsmouth, hopefully near the Naval Regional Medical Center. The Navy made the search somewhat easier by listing approved housing for military personnel. We quickly found and chose an approved apartment near the hospital. Our plan was to occupy the apartment prior to the movers arriving with our furniture and other belongings. We decided that we could afford a new car, so we traded our used 1973 Monte Carlo for a 1976 model. The new car had a rocket for an engine, aerodynamic styling, swivel bucket seats, a great radio with a tape player, and a hefty speaker system. With only a few days to spare, Brenda and I decided to drive to Birmingham and spend a few days with her parents, and then visit my grandparents in Chattanooga. Brenda's sister Elizabeth decided to accompany us to Portsmouth and help with the move. We were glad to have her company and assistance. I drove the Chevy Vega while Brenda and Elizabeth drove the Monte Carlo. The trip was scenic, the drive uneventful. We arrived in Portsmouth, took possession of the apartment, and waited for the arrival of the moving truck. Working as a team,

Brenda, Elizabeth, and I quickly arranged the furniture and finished unpacking efficiently merely one day before the start of my internship year.

I reported early for duty in my brand-new summer uniform. The obstetrics and gynecology department secretary gave me a wonderful surprise: since this was the bicentennial year, military personnel considered non-essential were granted extended time off to celebrate this historic milestone. The entire Tidewater area was home to a complex of large military bases, shipyards, and docks for naval ships including aircraft carriers. Extensive preparations for the celebration were underway everywhere. I visited the commissary and discovered that tickets were on sale for a big concert and celebration at the Portsmouth stadium, which would include fireworks. Earth, Wind, and Fire, probably one of the most popular music groups of my time (certainly one of my favorites), was scheduled to perform. I bought tickets and went home to tell Brenda, but she wasn't interested and told me to go enjoy myself. I'm sure she realized that I would not be having much fun the rest of the year. So I went alone, but thoroughly enjoyed every minute of the concert and fireworks. As I drove home after the concert, I smiled broadly, feeling content. I crawled into bed and cuddled with Brenda. In no time at all, both of us were fast asleep.

The morning of July fifth came much too soon. I was up by 5 a.m., as I was expected to be present in the hospital by 6 a.m. Again, I smiled as I made the drive to the hospital. There was something special about delivering a healthy baby and sharing the experience with the family. I proudly headed to the OB/GYN department, wearing my new white uniform and sporting my new lieutenant bars on my shoulders. The secretary directed me to the conference room where thirteen other doctors were seated. I found an empty chair and sat down. I couldn't help noticing the looks on all of their faces, many of them reddened. The room became extremely quiet. I had sat there for more than five minutes when the secretary came to rescue me. "Come with me, Dr. Ellis; I have some important paperwork you need to complete. Must get your pay started on time, don't you agree?"

"Yes, ma'am," I replied. "I need the paycheck!" I completed the paperwork rapidly and then returned to the conference room, where I found the chief resident speaking about duties and responsibilities. Since I had missed most of his remarks, I approached him at the end of his talk and explained that I was the new first-year resident. He spoke to me in a very abrupt manner, saying, "I don't have time to repeat myself. Go ask one of the other residents." With that, he turned and walked away.

It was more than obvious that I was not welcome. One of the reasons I had chosen the Navy of all the branches of the armed services was the recent promotion of an African American to the rank of admiral, the first black admiral ever. I had thought that the reputation of racism in the Navy was waning and Admiral Gravely was proof of that. However, the looks on the faces of my fellow residents led me to believe otherwise: racism was alive and well here.

My silence was broken by the voice of a fellow resident. "Okay, Dr. Ellis, why don't you take a look at your patients? Oh, by the way, my name is Patrick."

I replied, "Nice to meet you," as I extended my hand to shake his. He had a rather puzzled look on his face and did not reciprocate. Instead he said, "Let's get started; follow me."

Patrick was a second-year resident assigned as my supervisor. We methodically examined the twelve patients I was assigned. Most were pregnant with various medical issues such as diabetes and hypertension. They had been hospitalized to monitor the pregnancy for complications and to stabilize their systemic illnesses. There were also a few gynecology patients recovering from recent surgical procedures. Next, I was taken to the delivery ward, called the labor deck. Patients in labor were admitted for monitoring and to ensure safe delivery of the baby as well as the mother's wellbeing. Delivery suites and operating rooms were also located on this floor.

The first-year residents took night call on the labor ward every third night. Tomorrow night was the beginning of night call for me and the beginning of 110-120 hour work weeks. My day started at 6 a.m. and usually ended between 6 and 7 p.m. Night call coverage started at 6 p.m. The second-, third-, and fourth-year residents spent a lot of time performing surgery during the day, followed by surgical follow-up clinics. Teaching conferences were scheduled at noon every day. My first day ended with a brief meeting with the chairman of the department. I was surprised by his calm demeanor. He was the first person to welcome me to the department. I thought, *Maybe I'll have least one friend in this department.*

My drive home seemed unusually long as I contemplated my new responsibilities. I knew that Brenda would not like being alone so much. This was going to be a difficult year for us. Once I got home, I talked with Brenda about my schedule and adjustments we both needed to make. I thought it would be better for her to find employment rather than sit at home all day. Additionally, we both agreed that we needed to reach out more and find new friends. Brenda made an effort to find a job, and did so rather quickly. She was offered a special education position in Virginia Beach. I was thrilled that she found a spot so quickly, but after discussing this opportunity with her, it became apparent that she had some reservations. She said, "Jimmy, I don't feel comfortable driving fifteen miles to Virginia Beach every day. I would rather stay home and make life as comfortable for you as possible."

I thought about her comments and replied, "Well, after some thought, maybe you have a point. This year will be stressful enough with my schedule. I thought that it would help you manage the loneliness better if you were employed."

"I want to be here for you," she said. "You need to relax

once you get home, eat a nice meal, and enjoy the time we have together."

I smiled at her, warmly embraced her, and whispered softly, "Then that's what we'll do." That evening, Brenda prepared a wonderful dinner, which we followed by listening to our favorite music. Shortly thereafter, we both retired and quickly fell asleep in each other's arms.

The day my night call schedule commenced, my morning was uneventful, progressing quickly. All of my patients were stable, and a few were discharged. The morning clinic consisting of both obstetrics and gynecology patients was busy. There were three other upper-level residents to help staff the clinic. Some of these patients needed to be admitted to the hospital, while others were managed as outpatients. Following a brief lunch, I headed to the inpatient ward to perform histories and physicals on newly admitted patients. If appropriate, therapy or treatment was started. Afternoon patient rounds were conducted. Any patient needing special care or frequent checks by the physician was bought to the attention of the physician on call—in this case, me. At the end of the regular day, I reported to the labor and delivery floor, but I was stopped at the door by a very large and menacing nurse. She wore the rank of commander, so I stood at attention.

She addressed me, "Doctor, you must be clean-shaven to enter labor and delivery!" I had completely forgotten that I was sporting a goatee! Some facial hair was allowed in the Navy, but I was not going to disobey a superior officer. She directed me to a restroom, gave me a razor, and instructed me to shave off my goatee. I complied immediately. Once accomplished, I went to the surgical suites and received surgical scrubs to wear. Next, I proceeded to one of the surgical scrub sinks to undergo a thorough cleaning of my hands, arms, and face. Now I was ready to go to work, so I settled in to the on-call quarters. Basically, this was a room with a bed and a separate shower. After sitting in a comfortable chair for approximately five minutes, I made rounds on the patient's present. There were eight total patient rooms, each containing a patient in labor. Once I was satisfied that everyone was stable, I decided to grab a quick bite to eat and call Brenda. Food was sent to labor and delivery, as circumstances often were not conducive for a leisurely stroll to the cafeteria. My first delivery occurred around 8:30 that night: a single healthy baby delivered to the grateful parents! After returning from this delivery, two more patients had been admitted, one about to deliver even before we got her settled into her bed. So, back I went to the delivery and delivered my second baby. A third and fourth delivery followed quickly. I paused to check the time: only 11:30!

I was blessed with excellent nursing assistants. These nurses were so experienced that I believed that they really did not need me! It was quiet, so I retired to the on-call room to sleep. The nurses monitoring the remaining patients would awaken me if needed. I called Brenda to say goodnight, then quickly fell asleep. Approximately forty-five minutes passed quietly, and then all hell broke loose.

I was awakened and called *stat* to the admissions area. The patient en route was already in active labor with delivery reportedly imminent. As soon as I arrived, the doors at the entrance to labor and delivery burst open and a very pregnant lady shouted, "My baby is coming!" As soon as she uttered these words a gush of fluid ran down her legs, followed immediately by the baby! The infant hit the floor, still tethered to its mother by the umbilical cord! We all rushed to the patient's and baby's aid. Thankfully, the robust baby girl cried vigorously as soon as I touched her. Mom and baby did fine. Near the end of my internship, that mom came to visit me and show off her beautiful baby daughter! It was moments like that one that kept me going.

By the time a month had passed, I had settled into a good routine at the hospital. However, my colleagues continued to ostracize me, as did most of the attending physicians in the department. One exception was Dr. Hall, a Berry Plan physician. The Berry Plan was a Vietnam War-era recruiting plan for the armed forces. Drafting physicians during Vietnam was extremely unpopular, and ultimately caused a severe physician shortage for the troops. The Berry Plan allowed physicians to volunteer for two years of military service to satisfy their military service obligation. The plan worked; many talented physicians from prestigious institutions such as Johns Hopkins, Harvard, Massachusetts General Hospital, and Brigham and Woman's Hospital, helped train thousands of young doctors in the military. They served as attending physician staff at the prestigious military hospitals like Walter Reed, Bethesda Naval Hospital, and Balboa Naval Hospital in San Diego. The hospital at Portsmouth was also staffed with many of these Berry Plan doctors, all excellent. I was grateful that Dr. Hall was always supportive and encouraging. He was honest enough with me to acknowledge the cold treatment I was receiving from my fellow OB/GYN residents. There was no other rational reason for their behavior.

It was not long before most of the doctors, including residents who were assigned to the clinic, stopped showing up for their assignment when I was scheduled, which meant that I had to see all the patients that four residents and staff physicians usually saw. I seemed to have an unusual burden of complex patients to manage, usually without advice from my immediate supervisor who was a second-year resident or other senior residents. The other first-year resident seemed to have the support of all the other residents. He had a lighter patient load, plus he got more surgery time, which was critical to mastering OB/GYN surgical cases. Dr. Hall informed me that despite my unfair treatment, my patients received excellent care and I was considered to be excellent intern. However, because of this extensive workload I was more exhausted than the average intern. On several occasions, Brenda informed me that I had fallen asleep while eating my dinner. One time, she helped me clean up after my face landed in my plate.

I did get to participate (rarely) in surgical cases, but only as an assistant relegated to holding retractors. One memorable case involved the chief resident. The surgical procedure was going well when all of a sudden he threw one of the hemostats across the surgical suite, yelling at the top of his lungs, "Goddamn niggardly instrument!" As quickly as he uttered these words, he followed them up by saying, "Oh, I'm sorry Jim, I didn't mean to insult you!" The operating room went completely silent. Within an instant everyone's face turned beet red. No one wanted to look me in the eye. That was the last time I was allowed to participate or be involved in any surgical cases.

That evening I discussed the incident with Brenda. I had made up my mind that it was time for me to leave the OB/GYN residency, but Brenda advised me to stick with it, so I did. The unfair treatment and work burden continued unabated. Occasionally, I would overhear bits and pieces of conversations among the residents about their hatred of certain races. There was no question about their negative feelings concerning African Americans, but I was surprised to hear that their hatred of Filipinos was worse. Filipinos had been our allies during World War II. They fought bravely alongside American soldiers to defeat the Japanese and have a long history of service in the United States Navy. Yet, there was this intense hatred expressed by many white servicemen that defied explanation. One night while on call, I witnessed the practice of this hatred. A very ill pregnant Filipino woman was transferred from Guantánamo Bay in Cuba to the service at Portsmouth, prior to the start of my night call. My routine was to make rounds on the patients I would be caring for during the night. I discovered her behind a curtain in a corner on the ward; no nursing staff or doctors were caring for her. I was appalled that a pregnant human being was subjected to this abuse, the deliberate withholding of medical care! I immediately evaluated her, estimating that she was between twenty and twenty-two weeks pregnant. The fetal heart rate was 180-185 beats per minute. The mother's vital signs were normal except for slight fever. I was concerned that she may have the early signs of amnionitis, an intrauterine infection. I wrote orders to start treating her aggressively with intravenous antibiotics and instructed the nurses to inform me of any changes in the patient's condition. I then went over to labor and delivery to start my might call coverage. As usual, it was a busy night. It seemed that all of the pregnant women decided to go into labor that night. Whenever I got a chance between deliveries I called to get a status report on the Filipino patient. Her condition seemed to be improving. I reported this information to the supervising resident on call; he agreed that my treatment plan was appropriate. I got to rest briefly, around 5:30 a.m. At 6 a.m. I went to check on the Filipino patient and discovered her bed was empty! I went to the nursing station to inquire about her and I was ignored! I lost my composure and yelled, "What the hell happened? Why didn't anyone call me?"

One of the nurses replied, "The patient deteriorated rapidly and was taken to surgery. We were told not to awaken you. The mom and the baby died during surgery."

I was stunned! I quickly reviewed the recorded notes made during the night, and to my surprise, another order had been given by the senior resident to discontinue the antibody therapy I had started earlier. This order was given around midnight. I checked to make sure my notes and patient assessment were present in the medical record, and lo and behold, they were missing! One of my greatest character flaws was my naïveté about the goodness of man, that people were basically good. It amazed me to encounter such intense racial hatred. Early on in my career, I decided to make duplicates of all my patient encounters, doctor's notes, and doctor's orders for my records and as a teaching tool. Little did I know how valuable these records would prove to be. The missing record of my treatment of the Filipino patient was a huge red flag, a warning that something evil was heading my way.

That evening Brenda and I discussed my situation. She was not as surprised or stunned by the blatant racism; after all, she had grown up in George Wallace's Alabama. She had witnessed police dogs attack protest marchers and the use of fire hoses to dispel protesters. She knew the young girls killed in the church bombing in Birmingham. To her, what I was experiencing was expected. She suggested that I maintain my dignity, stay calm, and pray. I voiced my strong desire to transfer to another residency program, possibly in California. We retired to bed holding each other tight, not knowing what the next day would bring.

It started routinely, although somehow I sensed that all was not well. I was still shocked and dismayed by the previous night's events. I decided that I would talk to Dr. Cowan, the chief of obstetrics and gynecology, tell him what happened, and inform him that the medical record had been altered. I made it to his office just before noon. The secretary stated that he was meeting with the entire staff in the large conference room. I went to the conference room and it seemed that everyone was present; I was the last to arrive. Dr. Cowan started the meeting by announcing that this was a morbidity and mortality discussion. The subject? The pregnant Filipino patient. The senior resident assigned to the case presented his version of the course of events. He explained that the patient was assigned to him. He stated that before he left for the day the patient was stable and on antibiotics. As I listened, my anger started to build, as well as my fear. *That lying son of a bitch! They are trying to blame me for this patient's death!* Then the senior resident confirmed my fears, saying, "Dr. Ellis was the on-call intern and had refused to check on the patient. Further, Dr. Ellis gave an order to stop the antibiotic therapy." He went on to state that they all tried to save her life but because of my incompetence, the patient died, as well as the fetus. I was going to be the scapegoat!

Dr. Cowan turned to me and said, "Well, Dr. Ellis what do you have to say? It sounds like there may be grounds here for disciplinary action as well as a possible court-martial."

I remembered what Brenda had said to me last night, to keep my composure, maintain my dignity, and pray. My hand touched a small briefcase I carried with me at all times. It was a medical school graduation gift. Inside were reference books, patient history cards, and the duplicates of my doctor's notes and my doctor's orders for the Filipino patient. These documents were a direct contradiction of the senior resident's statements. He was lying and God knows who else was covering it up.

I stood to speak; the silence in the room was eerie. I told my version of the story, the real facts about the case and I spoke with conviction. I spoke about how I felt that the patient had been abandoned, relegated to a corner behind closed drapes, and left to die. There were no orders written for the patient, nor was there a physical examination present on the chart. I spoke about the blatant racial hatred I had overheard expressed by my fellow residents and most of the staff.

Cowan interrupted, "What proof do you have too support your version of the story? This is your word against virtually the entire department." He further stated that he believed the resident's story rather than mine, that I failed to follow the orders he had written for the patient, and that I did not fulfill my duties to see the patient while I was on call.

I took a long, slow breath. "Sir, I have duplicates of my progress notes, physical examination, and doctor's orders for the patient. I evaluated this patient while I was on call, made the diagnosis, and started treatment with intravenous antibiotics. I checked on this patient and it appeared that she was responding to antibiotics and improving. After I saw the patient, apparently someone ordered that the antibiotics be discontinued—but that decision did not come from me." I presented my documents, which were signed and dated by me and by the nurse who started the antibiotics. At that point a lot of faces turned bright red!

Dr. Cowan cleared his throat and spoke. "These documents are convincing. Someone is lying and I don't think it is Dr. Ellis! Good job, Dr. Ellis, and keep up the good work! This meeting is adjourned. I would like to meet with the resident in charge of this case in my office immediately!"

It occurred to me that if I wanted to leave the OB/GYN residency or transfer to another hospital with the same department, now was the time. That evening, Brenda and I discussed the day's events. She was thrilled that I had been vindicated, but we agreed that it would be healthier for me and for our marriage if I switched to another specialty. After a brief discussion, we agreed that radiology would be a good fit. My technical and engineering training in college had prepared me well for board certification in radiology; moreover my elective rotation on radiology in medical school was most productive and left me with a favorable impression of the specialty. I remembered how great a diagnostician Dr. Robinsky was. Additionally, I remained amazed at the amount of medical information a specialist like a radiologist could glean from an X-ray or radiograph. Lately I had read about the new technologies becoming available in radiology that would provide clearer images of human anatomy and pathologic conditions. No doubt, these technological advances would enhance the diagnostic capability and accuracy of radiologists. One of these new technologies was magnetic resonance imaging (MRI), which was familiar to me because of its scientific applications in chemistry. Specialties like radiology usually had very little night call, which appealed to Brenda and me.

I decided to switch my specialty from obstetrics and gynecology to radiology. To do so, I needed permission from the United States Medical Corps Office of Graduate Medical Education in Washington, DC. I drafted a letter stating that it would be mutually beneficial for the Medical Corps and for me because there was a shortage of specialists like radiologists in the Navy. Also, I pointed out that the Medical Corps would get three years of service from me while I was in training. Of course, the Navy would get an additional three years from me as I fulfilled my service for the payment of my medical school expenses. I also proposed that I could finish my internship as a rotating intern. A rotating internship was advantageous because of the exposure to the various medical specialties. I wanted a good basic experience in internal medicine, so I proposed spending four months practicing internal medicine, two months on the anesthesiology service, and one month each in pediatrics, radiology, gynecology, and general surgery. The two months I had already spent in the OB/GYN department counted for two months of obstetrics service. Additionally, I proposed that I continue to take my night call like usual every third night. However, I would be assigned to the emergency room when a specialty I was assigned to did not have a night call assignment for the rotating intern. To support my request, Dr. Hall was kind enough to write a letter of recommendation for me.

I was surprised at how quickly I received a response letter from the Department of Medical Education, granting me permission to make the changes that I had proposed! Brenda and I were ecstatic—the hell I was in changed to something better, something we both could live with. There was some backlash, however. The OB/GYN chief was not pleased, since my leaving would increase the workload for the remaining residents. I told him that my rotating internship did include one month on the gynecology service, which meant that I would get to be abused by manning the gynecology clinic alone. This seemed to pacify him somewhat. I had spent six weeks on the obstetrics service, delivered over 150 healthy babies, managed care for over 100 patients successfully, and established a reputation as a good, compassionate doctor with my patients. I would miss them but not the wretches who called themselves doctors. For the sake of humanity, I hoped that they would never get to practice again if it was God's will.

The remainder of 1976 was less stressful as I met other doctors who were dedicated to the practice of medicine and delivery of excellent medical care to all. My radiology rotation reconfirmed my decision to become a radiologist. The department chairman, Dr. Goodman, was kind and supportive. He recommended that I applied for the Navy radiology residency program in San Diego, California. This residency, considered one of the best in the Navy, was located at Balboa Naval Hospital, part of the Naval Regional Medical Center in San Diego. San Diego was home to the 11th Naval District, the largest in the world. In 1976, the Naval Hospital radiology department performed over 400,000 exams. San Diego had a very large active-duty and retiree population. So the patients requiring medical treatment and radiology services were diverse ranging from newborns to the elderly. The residency program included rotations at the University of California San Diego radiology residency program, considered one of the best in the country. Near the end of my one-month radiology rotation, I received confirmation that I was going to San Diego for a radiology residency.

The following two months, I was assigned to the anesthesia service. I enjoyed the experience and the patients I cared for. My background in chemistry helped me better understand the pharmacology of the drugs I used. The anesthesia staff thought that I was talented enough to enter the anesthesia residency. I was flattered but decided to stick with my decision to pursue radiology. Funnily enough, I met an African American anesthesia intern! It was great to meet another brother. Dr. Anthony Goforth hailed from Jacksonville, Florida. Although he too had had his share of racially related incidents in the Navy, his spirit was undiminished. A jovial person, his broad, hearty laughter elevated my spirit. I don't ever recall seeing him frown or express anger. He was one of the brightest and most dedicated young physicians I've had the privilege of meeting. He and his wife Phyllis became instant friends of Brenda and me. We also discovered that all of us were headed to San Diego, California, for residency training, Anthony for anesthesiology and I radiology. For the remainder of the internship we all enjoyed the rare opportunities we had to socialize.

1977 started badly. Brenda's father passed in January. Mr. Harris was a quiet stately gentleman who walked erect and always looked you in the eye. He never smiled much but I knew I was welcome in his home. He had moved from rural Bullock County to Birmingham with his wife and built a brick ranch style home literally with his bare hands, where they created a comfortable middle-class life for their family. He was loved and revered by family and a multitude of friends. Brenda felt his loss very deeply. Medical school and internship had taken its toll on our relationship, making Brenda seem bitter and unhappy, but the passing of her father bought us closer. We tried as often as possible to spend time alone to comfort and hold each other. Death has a sobering effect, reminding us of how tenuous life is, reminding us of our own mortality. Brenda began to attend church on Sunday with her new friend Phyllis. I always seemed to be on call or attending to other patient duties at the hospital most Sundays. I was happy that she was not isolated. Going to church appeared to elevate her mood and improve her energy level.

The month of February, although cold, bought some needed warmth to our lives. It was time for me to take my licensing exam in Richmond. I was excited because I would get a chance to visit with my favorite teacher, Mrs. Epps, with whom I had kept in touch on a regular basis. I informed her that I would be in Richmond, and if possible I would like her to meet my wife Brenda. Mrs. Epps invited Brenda and me to her home for dinner, and of course I accepted!

The licensing exam went well although I felt that my concentration was somewhat diminished because all I could think about was seeing my favorite teacher again. Mrs. Epps welcomed Brenda and me warmly as we entered her home. What a surprise also to see my eighth-grade guidance counselor, Mrs. Holmes! It was due to her persistent efforts that I got the opportunity to go to Cushing Academy. I was thrilled that Brenda finally got to meet the two most influential people in my life about whom she had heard so much. We had a wonderful dinner and plenty of conversation about all of our lives since we had last seen each other. As Brenda and I were leaving to return to Portsmouth, I promised that I would not let another twelve years elapse before seeing them again. We said our goodbyes. I could tell by the look Mrs. Holmes and Mrs. Epps gave me that they both were extremely proud of me.

Winter quickly gave way to spring. By mid-March, all the snow had melted and signs of life were beginning to appear. Flowers were sprouting, birds were singing, grass was turning green, flowering trees perfumed the air. The sunshine was invigorating. Soon, internship would end and I would start my specialty training in radiology in San Diego. I had survived the craziest year of my life, been tested mentally and physically, and passed—but at a cost. Brenda told me she could not endure another year like this one; she was tired of being second in my life, tired of sitting at home waiting for me. I was stunned. I thought that of all people that she would be my greatest supporter, that she understood the sacrifices involved now would pay huge dividends in the future—a very bright future for us. However, our discussion became more heated, and our conversation escalated into a serious argument. Finally, I told her that if she wanted out of the marriage, she should not accompany me to San Diego. As quickly as I said that I wished I had not. Our argument ceased abruptly. We barely spoke to each other for weeks. The warmth of spring could not thaw the frosty air between us. For the first time ever, I started to have serious doubts about the soundness of our marriage, and its survival.

Finally, my internship year ended. I felt like a seasoned doctor, able to diagnose and treat any ill patient entering the hospital or emergency room. However, I was tired and needed a break. I had lost thirty-five pounds; I was weak and needed to sleep, to rest. In fact, I felt that if I fell asleep, I could easily sleep twenty-four to thirty-six hours. I had not used any of the thirty allotted vacation days during internship, so I decided to use it now, not only to rest but also to help repair and reinvigorate my marriage. Brenda and I agreed to return to Birmingham for most of that vacation. I also found time to visit Granddaddy and Big Mama and my siblings in Chattanooga. Being in the nurturing environment of home, around family and friends, was just the therapy our marriage needed. It was truly a real honeymoon, and much needed, as we had never had one.

Prior to traveling to San Diego, Brenda and I located a rental house in Poway, a small town just north of the city. The home was on the Navy's list of approved housing. Rested, nourished, and recommitted, Brenda and I began the drive to San Diego. We drove the Monte Carlo with the Chevy Vega in tow along Interstate 10. The green hills of Texas changed to desert in New Mexico, where the temperature soared, reaching 117 degrees as we passed through Las Cruces. We traveled on through Arizona, and ahead lay the mountains we needed to cross to reach San Diego. A twinge of fear passed through me as I fretted about the integrity of the tow bar. I briefly closed my eyes and ask for God's protection, then continued with determination, knowing that I would not fail.

CHAPTER 5

Residency

San Diego appeared as an ocean-side oasis once we reached the peak of the mountains east of the city. We had been driving for some time on Interstate 8, passing through El Cajon, and then switching to Interstate 15 north for the short drive to Poway, California. We found our rental home easily. It was a three-bedroom ranch house, nicely furnished, with easy access to the freeway for the trip south to San Diego. The neighborhood was extremely nice, more upscale than I thought it would be. I was able to afford the rent because the Navy subsidized my housing allowance; San Diego had a very high cost-of-living index. The neighbors were friendly; in fact, the people we met seemed always to be smiling, whether they were native Californians or not. I thought, *Maybe it's the perfect weather that makes everyone so pleasant.* The daytime temperature almost always was near seventy-two degrees, slightly cooler on the coast. Nighttime temperatures were near fifty. That explained why our house did not have air conditioning. In fact, no one we spoke to had air conditioning! The night before I was to report for duty, Brenda and I relaxed, ate dinner, and then sat in our new back yard, gazing at the clear night sky filled with stars. I sensed that we both felt that this was as happy as we had been in a long while.

I arose early, donned my new uniform, and started the drive south along Interstate 15 to report for duty at Balboa Naval Hospital. I drove past the exit for Miramar Naval Air Station, about a ten-minute drive south. The air station contained a very large commissary selling groceries and clothing at prices far lower than at the civilian stores. Further south was the Naval Regional Medical Center and Balboa Naval Hospital, where I would begin my radiology residency. In California, residents described driving distance in terms of minutes rather than miles. Everyone assumed the average traveling speed was sixty miles per hour, although you actually had to drive at seventy because no one really traveled at sixty on California freeways!

I parked in the main parking lot. The hospital overlooked San Diego's harbor, so I paused to take in the panoramic view. The hospital complex consisted of numerous pink stucco buildings built in the early 1900s. The harbor, busy with military and commercial ship traffic, seemed to shimmer and glisten in the early morning sunlight. There was no fog bank this morning; Point Loma was visible in the distance. The Coronado Bay Bridge, a beautiful structure, descended to famed Coronado Island. *Damn*, I thought, *this place is the closest thing to heaven on earth I have ever seen!*

I shook off my wonder and proceeded into the administration building to ask for directions to the radiology department. I was quickly directed to a larger and newer building: the main hospital. I met the department chairman, Dr. Fred Gavin. He was an ex-Marine, fit, tanned, and sporting a trimmed black beard. With a friendly demeanor, he articulated his thoughts clearly, detailing expectations of me that amounted to nothing short of excellence. He also encouraged me to consider purchasing a home! I thought, *I can't afford a home; I'm just a first-year resident!* I was about to say as much when Dr. Gavin explained that real estate prices were crazy here; prices rose every day with potential buyers on waiting lists. Homes sold for full price, and occasionally there were bidding wars for property! He further explained that the G.I. Bill made home purchasing easy, usually forgoing a down payment. The additional housing allowance provided by the Navy made a mortgage affordable. I felt that his reasoning was sound. He had convinced me to seriously consider purchasing a home. I could not wait until I arrived home to tell Brenda that we were going to buy a house!

Dr. Gavin escorted me to the main radiology department, where I was introduced to the staff doctors responsible for supervision and training of the radiology residents. Also, I met all of the radiology residents—eleven besides me. I was the last resident to report for duty. Dr. Gavin excused himself, leaving me in the hands of the supervising staff. I was called aside by Dr. David Hart. He was not happy! He launched into a mild tirade, "Well, where have you been? The residency started July 1! Why are you late?"

I replied, "Sir, I took some time off to move from Virginia to California. Additionally, I did not take any vacation time during my entire internship."

Dr. Hart responded, "Didn't you get my letter specifically telling you to report for duty by July 1? In order to qualify for taking the written part of the radiology board certification examination, the American College of Radiology requires candidates to have completed twenty-four months of residency training. Since you are late reporting, you can't take the written examination until near the completion of your residency! Individuals who delay taking the written board examination usually perform poorly on the oral portion of the board certification examination; the odds are against you becoming board-certified!"

I was furious! How dare anyone speak to me in such a way! The competitive fire within me ignited. *I'll show you. I'll prove you wrong!* However, I stuffed my explosive feelings and replied meekly, "I am very sorry sir. I will do my best." Dr. Gavin then proceeded to recite a lengthy list of responsibilities including a must-read list of radiology books and journals. Afterward, I stood alone for several minutes before another staff radiologist approached me.

Dr. Lawrence Applegate pulled me aside. "Don't worry, Dr. Ellis, you'll be fine. Come with me; let's get started. I'll show you how to use the fluoroscope and perform barium studies, which will be your primary responsibility for the first six months of residency."

I had been introduced to the fluoroscope during my one-month rotation on radiology during my internship. This equipment allowed the radiologist to see inside the patient. Important findings seen during the examination were recorded on radiographs that were interpreted on the view box, an illuminated fourteen-by-seventeen-inch panel used to view X-rays and other tests. Before this upgraded version of fluoroscopic equipment was introduced, the radiologist had to "dark adapt"; that is, one's visual acuity had to adapt to the total darkness in which the fluoroscopic examination was performed. During fluoroscopy, the radiologist wore a lead apron for protection against the repeated exposure to ionizing radiation. A dosimeter badge was worn by all radiology workers to monitor exposure and ensure that no one was exposed to too much radiation.

Dr. Applegate gave a brief tutorial on how to perform the fluoroscopic exams, what to look for, and how to record radiographs. After thirty minutes, I was performing these exams under direct supervision. By the end of the week I was working alone. By the end of the first month I could perform twenty barium studies between 7:30 a.m. and 11:30 a.m. In other exam rooms, non-barium radiology studies such as bronchograms, intravenous pyelograms, myelograms, arthrograms, and biopsies were performed. Usually, more senior residents performed these other tests. The afternoons were spent interpreting the tests with the supervising staff radiologists. Final radiology reports were dictated, signed, and sent back to the referring physician as quickly as possible. Trained radiology technicians performed numerous other radiology studies throughout the day; residents interpreted these radiographs as well, with the supervising staff.

Teaching conferences occurred at noon. Radiology residents were challenged with unknown cases and asked to interpret them correctly. As expected, the more senior radiology residents performed better than their junior peers. My fellow first-year peers had a distinctive advantage over me, thanks to having spent their entire internship year in radiology. They were essentially second-year residents by experience; I was referred to as the only true first-year resident because my knowledge of radiology was at least one year behind theirs. Initially, I was intimidated and felt overwhelmed. However, I settled down and began doing what I had to do to catch up—study, study, study. Dr. Hart approached me after one of my embarrassing conference performances with his recommendation for a plan of study. He explained how he studied by outlining material and recording key information on index cards, which he used later as a study aid. He kept all of his note cards so that when it was time to review, the information was readily available in a compact concise form. I immediately began using this technique and to my surprise, it worked! I began to close the knowledge gap quickly. I used this technique successfully for many years.

Brenda and I seemed closer than at any point in our marriage. The punishing life of an intern was over for me; I felt human again. I began to gain weight, and my health improved because I had time to eat properly and exercise—and sleep. After a year of constant sleep deprivation, my body and brain got some severely needed rest. Radiology night call was once a week. Usually after 11 p.m., the radiology resident got to sleep undisturbed until 5 a.m.

Brenda was eager to get pregnant, so we began trying in earnest. She conceived after one month of trying. I was going to be a daddy! Brenda and I discussed purchasing a home. Our research confirmed that purchasing a home in San Diego made good sense financially. We realized that we could purchase a new home with no money down using the G.I. Bill benefits. The mortgage would be subsidized by an additional housing allowance provided by the Navy. In no time at all we found the perfect home, in a new subdivision, Mira Mesa, which was closer to the hospital and adjacent to Miramar Naval Air Station. This was convenient because we would be less than two miles away from shopping at the large commissary. Our new home had three bedrooms, two bathrooms, and was fully landscaped with sprinklers. The lawn was a lush dark green; a groundcover called ice plant (succulent variety) filled the rear of the sloped back yard; the front yard contained a palm tree. The entrance to the home was lined with other succulent plants and a cluster of camellias that produced wonderfully fragrant light-pink flowers. Brenda and I purchased our home for $59,900. Next, we bought furniture for the master bedroom, living room, and a dinette set for the kitchen. That first night in our new home with our unborn child, lying on our new bed, gave Brenda and I a giddy feeling. We were holding hands and looked at each other, smiling broadly. *This is as good as it gets for a young doctor in training and his family.*

I loved my routine. I awakened before sunrise, exercised, and then ate breakfast. With a big hug and kiss for Brenda, I was out the door to the Naval Hospital. My commute was about fifteen minutes shorter, which was great. Once I arrived in the radiology department, I discovered that my friend Anthony and his wife Phyllis had left a message for me with the department secretary. They had been assigned to San Diego Naval Hospital and had just arrived! I contacted Anthony and invited him and his wife Phyllis to visit us Friday evening. They bought a couple of friends with them, which we did not mind; we all had a wonderful Friday telling stories, listening to music, playing card games, and eating plenty of pizza. I encouraged Anthony to purchased a home, but he felt it was too risky. He and Phyllis decided to rent for a while.

Anthony was completely satisfied with his anesthesia residency. Everyone seemed friendly, courteous, and helpful. Brenda and I met other civilian doctors and lawyers practicing in San Diego who encouraged us to remain once my military obligation was completed. It soon became routine for all of us to meet at someone's home one night of the weekend to relax and socialize. All of these social gatherings were exclusively African American. It was rare for me to be invited to the home of any of the staff radiologists or other residents in the radiology department. One exception was a second-year resident named Foster Kim, whose wife was also a physician practicing in the Navy. Foster invited me to go sailing with him on San Diego Bay. Thoughts of Rochester New York and my frightening experience sailing in the catamaran boat with Elmer flashed through my mind; however, I thought I would give it another try. I was rewarded; the water was absolutely calm and the views were spectacular, with the San Diego skyline appearing to rise up out of the bay.

Foster and his wife lived on Coronado Island, famous for the Coronado Hotel. He was the only radiology resident who talked to me about issues other than medicine or radiology. He shared details about growing up in foster homes. I think he felt that I, more than others, understood his background. We both knew what real poverty and deprivation were like, and so we both appreciated our current lives and opportunities. Still, at times, he appeared withdrawn and unhappy. His mood seemed to darken when the rainy season started. Everyone thought that he would recover once his sailing could resume in earnest. Sadly, it was not to be. I don't remember the exact date because I tried to put this memory out of my conscious mind. On a rainy day in February of 1978, the radiology department received the horrible news of Foster's suicide. For me, it was like a punch in the gut. I wondered if I could have done or said anything to help him. I felt that when he had needed a friend the most, I had missed an opportunity to be there for him. To this day I still think of him.

Brenda's oldest sibling, her brother Johnny, had moved to Los Angeles, California, in the early '60s; she hadn't seen him since she was a little girl. Brenda and I were in immediate contact with him and his wife Martha shortly after our move to San Diego. The first reunion was joyous. He pulled me aside and said, "Take care of my baby sister." He was delighted to see her pregnant and happily married. We all spent many weekends together enjoying each other's company.

On May 19, 1978, our daughter Courtney Elizabeth Ellis arrived, weighing seven pounds, eight ounces. Brenda's mother stayed with us for six weeks as Brenda and I were clueless new parents. Courtney was a very demanding baby, and we needed an extra pair of hands and the wisdom Mrs. Harris provided, not to mention the delicious meals she cooked for us. Courtney needed supplemental food early; her appetite was healthy, and she grew rapidly. One of my favorite pictures of Courtney was taken on Thanksgiving Day. We were enjoying dinner at Johnny's home in Los Angeles. Courtney, who was six months old, let it be known that she wanted to participate in the feast. She was in a walking trainer and positioned herself next to me, then started crying loudly. We all were puzzled at first, as she had eaten well just before dinner. She started reaching and actually begging for food. I had a very large turkey leg bone that she eagerly accepted and began gumming it enthusiastically!

From my perspective, my development as a radiology resident progressed well. However, I sensed the opposite from my peers. I felt ostracized, overhearing derogatory comments about me from my peers on many occasions. During one of my busy mornings, I was confronted by a pair of surgery residents who where checking on their patients in radiology. One of them snorted, "I guess they'll allow anyone to perform radiology these days. Times must be pretty bad if they're accepting baboons!"

I quickly snapped, "You should be worried; if baboons can perform radiology, they must be smarter than you!" There was silence, then reddened faces as they both turned quickly and stormed out of the radiology department. This encounter did not discourage me; if anything, it made me more resolute to become the best radiologist possible. I read all the major radiology textbooks and subspecialty books, and developed an interest in the newer radiology imaging technologies such as ultrasound and computed tomography (CT) scan. My peers believed that these new technologies would never gain much of an advantage over current imaging methods, but it was readily apparent to me that it was only a matter of time before these new imaging technologies replaced the old. Ultrasound and CT produced a clearer and more realistic depiction of internal human anatomy; you could actually see the internal organs and their surroundings with these new modalities. There was no doubt that these new tools would significantly impact radiology: diagnostic accuracy would improve, leading to better patient care. So, I studied these developing technologies in detail and became proficient using them. The other residents avoided using or learning how to interpret images produced by these technologies. I got to do as much ultrasound and CT interpretation as I wanted. My peers wanted as much experience as possible performing angiography, an advantage when one is trying to enter private practice.

By January 1979 I had reached the point in the residency when residents in radiology were sent to Washington D.C. for additional in-depth training in radiological physics. The course at Bethesda Naval Hospital would last two weeks. At the end of this course, I was scheduled to return to San Diego for approximately one week, then scheduled to go back to D.C. for a four-week course in radiology pathology at the Armed Forces Institute of Pathology (AFIP). Brenda was not happy that I'd be gone several weeks, and nor was I, but it was necessary to complete my radiology residency. Several days prior to leaving, Anthony and Phyllis stopped by to wish me a safe trip and to check on Brenda and Courtney. Anthony and I were laughing and telling jokes in the living room while Brenda and Phyllis talked in an adjacent bedroom. Brenda's voice seemed amplified, so Anthony and I stopped talking. We clearly heard Brenda talking to Phyllis about someone she had met while in Virginia who was trying to arrange a rendezvous with her in Los Angeles while I was out of town—and she was thinking about trying to meet him. I was stunned! Anthony put his hand on my shoulder and told me to remain calm when I confronted Brenda. Anthony suggested that he and Phyllis leave immediately, and they did.

Once Courtney had been put to bed, I confronted Brenda about the conversation I overheard. At first, she denied any relationship with another man. Once she realized that Anthony was a witness, she confessed, telling me what I dreaded to hear: she admitted to having had a brief affair with someone she met while I interned in Portsmouth. I was puzzled and asked how she met the man, assuming that she never left the apartment when I was away at the hospital. She told me that Phyllis had suggested that Brenda accompany her to a nightclub she frequented in Norfolk during weekends when Anthony was on call. She said she went along one of those weekend nights when I was on call too. She lied at first about the extent of this relationship but finally admitted that it had been sexual, and there had been multiple liaisons between January and June during my internship. Apparently Brenda and this man kept in touch frequently. After hearing all of this, I was overwhelmed with emotion, and slowly sank to the ground crying. I felt other emotions: anger, fear, depression, jealousy, hatred, pain. For me, this was the ultimate betrayal. All that I had believed about the institution of marriage and the values that I thought Brenda and I shared were severely fractured. I slept by myself that night, awakening numerous times, my brain swirling with unresolved emotions and disillusionment. I was a mess, but I had to leave for Washington in the morning.

The nonstop flight from San Diego to Washington lasted over four hours. During that time I tried to process my feelings but instead decided to suppress them deep into my subconscious in a place I called the dark room with the door closed. This was my coping mechanism. I closed my eyes and took myself back to the memory of that perfect spring day, lying on the lush green carpet of grass in my backyard in Richmond. It was like utopia, seeing and enjoying all the sights and senses nature presented to me. This was my safe place to return to during troubled times for rest and peace and healing. I returned often to this place during this crisis.

I pushed my personal problems aside once I arrived at Bethesda Naval Hospital. The two-week didactic instructional course was well-organized. This course was mandatory for all radiology residents in military and civilian training programs. The physics and mathematics courses were a good review for me as I had prior exposure at WPI. I performed well. At least I was good at something: studying, learning, and taking tests. However, I could not help but think about the state of my personal life. I felt like a failure. The course ended and I returned to San Diego for one week. We decided that it would be better for Brenda to be in Birmingham with her family so that she could get help with Courtney. They would remain in Birmingham until my instructional courses at the AFIP concluded. Brenda and I were as far apart as ever. I wanted a divorce but could not stand the thought of being apart from my precious daughter, Courtney. Maybe the four weeks in Washington would help me sort out the mess of my personal life.

The AFIP course was mandatory for all military radiology residents and for many of the civilian radiology training programs. There were well over one hundred residents in attendance for this course, which was held in the AFIP auditorium equipped with state-of-the-art audiovisual aids. Every seat in the auditorium was positioned to maximize viewing of presented material. Course instructors invited to lecture at AFIP were considered the best in radiology. Many received additional stipends to study in their chosen area of expertise in radiology. Each resident attending AFIP was required to bring an unusual or rare case of known pathology including the gross specimen and any X-rays or other images. Any pathology slides associated with the case were also required. I contributed an unusual case of xanthogranulomatous pyelonephritis. Case contributions by the residents were an excellent way for AFIP to maintain a file of unusual but instructional cases to share with all radiologists. The institute's teaching mission was to show residents how radiology correlated with gross pathology. One term used to describe radiology was that the specialty provided *in vivo* pathology. Radiographs of gross specimens when correlated with the pathologic appearance of the specimen were so strikingly similar! Remembering the correlation helped me with my diagnostic accuracy. The four weeks I spent studying at AFIP marked a turning point, a transition in my radiology education and confidence level. All of the reading and studying I had previously done started to make sense to me. I returned to San Diego relaxed and exuding confidence, excited to see my little daughter.

Brenda and Courtney had already returned when I arrived home. Courtney did not recognize me at first and treated me like a stranger. She turned her head away from me and would not let me hold her. Two minutes passed; then she turned her head, looked at me out of the corner of her eye, and smiled and reached for me to hold her. We both hugged for what seemed like an eternity. Brenda appeared thinner and unhappy. She did not speak or talk very much. I had decided to divorce her while I was in Washington; I did not want to continue a marriage in which I was unhappy. Prior to filing divorce papers, my attorney suggested that we attend marriage counseling. Brenda became extremely uncooperative, refusing to attend counseling but also refusing to sign divorce papers. I became furious and resentful. I wanted revenge! The woman I had chosen to be my wife had hurt me to the core of my soul. I felt alone, betrayed. Something inside of me screamed, "You are sleeping with the enemy! Get out!"

I walked into Courtney's bedroom and stared at her while she slept, and I sensed a deep conflict within me. How could I leave my precious daughter to an uncertain future? I had always promised myself that I would not ever abandon my kids. I wanted to stay in Courtney's life as her father and give her all that she deserved. I went into the living room and sat on the couch most of the night. Finally, I decided to remain at home.

Several weeks passed. I wanted to have some fun. It was 1979; the disco era and club scene dominated San Diego night life. I was curious to see why people paid money to stay up late into the night and dance. One evening, I decided to go to a club called Maxi's, a popular disco club. I paid the exorbitant ten-dollar cover charge and entered into a fantasy world! Everyone was friendly and seemed to be having the time of their lives. I learned a new dance called "the Rock." I must say that I thought it was illegal to have this much fun! I arrived home by midnight and promptly fell asleep.

I became a regular at Maxi's every Thursday night. I really was not interested in pursuing anyone romantically; I just wanted to enjoy myself and release some stress. Regardless, many women offered me their phone numbers and I promptly threw most of them away … except for one. Amy was different. I sensed that she knew that I was lonely and hurting. She was extremely attractive, cerebral, and very wealthy. I enjoyed dancing and talking with her. Her family lived in Seattle, Washington, where her father was a highly successful real estate investor. Amy was a graduate student at UCSD (University of

California San Diego), studying for a PhD in psychology. She intended to stay in San Diego to practice psychology after she obtained her doctorate. I enjoyed dancing with her so much that I decided to take dancing lessons to impress her, as she was a talented dancer. We met at Maxi's every Thursday night to dance, and dance we did! We even entered several disco contests at Maxi's and won twice! We always left Maxi's at midnight. I would walk her to her car, hug, and then go our separate ways.

One Thursday evening, Amy called me at the hospital to tell me that she did not want to go to Maxi's. Instead, she invited me to her townhouse on Coronado Island for dinner. She greeted me with a hug and offered me a glass of champagne, which I eagerly accepted. We proceeded to her balcony to view the truly magnificent sunset. Jazz music was playing softly in the background. I was face-to-face with a beautiful woman, who had become a dear friend, gazing into my eyes! We embraced. I began to tingle all over. She had that look; I knew that I was in trouble, but didn't care. We seemed to float from the balcony to the living room, to the shower, then to her bed, covered with rose petals and satin sheets. For the next two hours I traveled to a timeless place of pure ecstasy. We ended up right where we started, on the balcony. We stood on her balcony holding each other tight, staring at the stars and the San Diego skyline. Then we gazed at each other, kissed, and said our goodbyes. I arrived home before midnight. I went immediately to Courtney's room and looked at her sleeping. Suddenly she opened her eyes raised her arms and smiled, saying, "Daddy! Daddy!" I picked her up; she clung to my neck. I kissed her and put her back in her bed; she promptly closed her eyes and fell asleep. Brenda and I were sleeping separately, so I entered the spare bedroom and fell fast asleep, still tingling.

The residency was progressing well for me. I was performing better and the department chairman and staff noticed; my fellow residents were at least speaking to me. The remainder of 1979 passed quickly. The end of July marked the beginning of my third and final year of residency. My personal life, though complex, was stable. Brenda and I continued sleeping in separate beds. I thoroughly enjoyed playing and reading to my daughter—she was my joy. I recognized early that she was extremely bright. She started to read to me before she was sixteen months old! When she was about eighteen months old I took her for a ride into San Diego. She hated staying in her car seat, always saying no when I asked her to comply. She preferred standing on the back seat to see out the back window of the car. I decided to drive through an area that had lots of signs to test her word recognition, and honestly, I would've been perfectly happy if she recognized the stop signs. Not only did she recognize the stop signs but also proceeded to lecture me about the stoplight. "Daddy, red means stop and green means go." I was amazed. Then she started pointing to the many signs with the names of car dealerships and announcing, "That sign says 'Chevy'; that sign says 'Ford.'" I was more than amazed! I hurried home to tell Brenda. At first, she didn't believe me, so we both got back into the car with Courtney and drove around to test her ability. Brenda immediately saw I hadn't been making it up!

That night while reading to Courtney, I start to fall asleep. She took the book away from me and began to read it aloud. This was the beginning of a lifelong love of learning and reading for Courtney. I realized I needed to be present to secure my daughter's future, to witness her development and provide all the tools she needed to succeed. I decided not to serve Brenda with divorce papers, and in return, she said she wanted us to reconcile and move forward. I agreed. I moved back into the master bedroom. Shortly thereafter Brenda became pregnant. I was surprised because I thought that she had an IUD in place. Later, she informed me that she had had it removed.

New Year's Day 1980 marked a new beginning, a new decade of hope. For America, the '70s was a decade of ineptitude. Vietnam was the first war that America felt that it had lost. Over fifty thousand American servicemen lost their lives, yet South Vietnam became a communist state anyway, uniting with North Vietnam. The Arab oil embargo exposed America's huge dependency on foreign oil for its energy needs. The economy stuttered under the 1973–74 recession. Religious nationalists attacked the American Embassy in Iran and took Americans hostage. A special forces raid to free the hostages failed miserably. Everyone's faith in government was shattered by the Watergate scandal that led to the resignation of Nixon. On top of all that, in 1979, I lost one of the most positive influences in my life with the passing of my grandfather. Most of my relatives say that I inherited his quiet reserve and compassionate demeanor. I could always detect that quiet look of approval in his eyes whenever he looked at me. He was extremely proud that his grandson was a doctor. I was extremely proud that he was my grandfather.

By mid-1980 my personal life started to improve. I wanted my marriage to work; I wanted my kids to have a father. I decided to discontinue the relationship with Amy; we both agreed that it was best if I wanted to stay married. On June 17, 1980, I was blessed with the birth of our son, James Van. Proud to have a son, I gave him my nickname, Van. I sensed that Courtney, accustomed to receiving all of the attention at home, seemed jealous of her new baby brother, so I was careful not to leave Van unattended for any period of time. Van, on the other hand, was not as demanding as his big sister had been as a baby. He started to sleep through the night earlier than we expected, and was generally easy-going. I adored both of my children, and became the quintessential doting father.

My residency training ended July 28, 1980. I was a bona fide radiologist! Unfortunately, I was not eligible to take my written board certification exam because I had not completed the required twenty-four months of residency by the cutoff date. The department chair, Dr. Gavin, asked me to remain in San Diego as a staff radiologist in the department. He felt that my chances of passing board certification examinations would improve if I remained in an academic environment. I was honored that he asked me to be part of the teaching staff, and it would definitely allow me more time to study for the certification exams. In October, I took the two-day written certification exam, passing all of it, including physics. The next and final scheduled certification exam was the oral section, considered the largest hurdle to certification. The American College of Radiology held the orals in Louisville, Kentucky, every year, usually during the first week of June. I prepared for this exam as if my life depended on passing it. For me to have any credibility among other radiologists, I had to become board-certified, and do so on the first try. I proceeded to get into the best shape of my life by running three to five miles every morning. On the weekends I would study by the ocean, usually in La Jolla. The cool ocean breezes and the sound of the surf crashing into the rocky shoreline seemed to enhance my concentration.

By the time my examination date arrived, I was tired of studying. Candidates for certification were examined in each subspecialty of radiology. The examiner for a particular subspecialty would present the candidate with unknown cases to diagnose and discuss other possible diagnoses. Any question the examiner wanted to ask of the candidate was fair game, including questions concerning pathophysiology as well as treatment, when appropriate. After the test, I felt as if a huge weight had been lifted from my shoulders. I returned home, knowing that I had given my all and praying that it was enough to pass. Waiting for the results was hard; I could not concentrate or sleep. I chose to receive my results at the hospital where everyone had their own personal mailbox. A week later, my heart pounded when I opened my box and found inside a letter from the American College of Radiology. I opened it with my eyes closed, then opened them and stared at the content of the letter. *Congratulations! You've passed. You are now a board-certified radiologist.*

I smiled, held my head high and my body erect, and entered the radiology department. No one asked me how I did. I am sure that the assumption was that I had failed. I approached Dr. Parrish to show him my letter. Dr. Parrish was near my age and had been recently certified, had given me advice about what I should study and often encouraged me. I thought he was one of the few in the radiology department that believed I could pass the rigorous examinations. I showed him the letter containing the good news of my success. To my surprise, he snatched the letter from me and tossed it on the floor after reading it! He then turned his back to me and continued working! *Wow,* I realized. *All of these jerks were expecting me to fail*! My immediate reaction was confusion, but it quickly changed to disgust! Indignant, I marched to the department chairman's office.

Before I could utter a word, Dr. Gavin said, "Hello, Dr. Ellis; how did you do?" I handed my letter to him, with the content clearly visible. He smiled immediately, jumped to his feet and gave me a hearty handshake. "Congratulations! I knew you could do it!"

I responded, "Thank you, sir! But why the cold reception from everyone else?"

He replied, "Jim, human nature being what it is, I am sure that an element of jealousy may explain some of that. However, I don't deny that there is some racism involved also. The premise is that African Americans are not smart enough to pass the radiology board examinations, and if they do, it is after taking the exams multiple times. Then, there you are standing in front of them in the flesh, a smart black doctor passing the board exams on the first try. They didn't expect you to pass on the first attempt, Jim. I did, though. I just knew you would. While you're here, I can call a friend at the American College of Radiology to get your scores if you're interested."

Dr. Gavin called and got the information quickly. He hung up the phone, smiled and said, "Well, Jim, you not only got the highest scores of any resident tested the same day you tested, but you also received the highest scores of any of our residents taking the exam! Congratulations on a job well done! I would love for you to stay here in San Diego as a member of this department."

I smiled, "That would be quite an honor. I need to discuss this matter further with Brenda. I will have an answer in the morning if that's okay."

That evening, Brenda and I discussed whether we should remain in San Diego or return to Memphis. Memphis was close to Birmingham, Chattanooga, and Richmond. The cost of living was lower than in San Diego. I also thought that job opportunities for me would be better in Memphis, with a chance to start my own radiology practice. I still had two years of obligatory military service, so I would have to move to a military hospital or base close to Memphis. The Navy had a facility at Millington, Tennessee. I had called the two radiologists stationed there, one of whom I would replace, earlier in the week, prior to my conversation with Dr. Gavin. I had asked about moonlighting opportunities in the Memphis area. I also had forwarded my CV. I received a positive response from both of them; they said there was plenty of moonlighting available and that they would recommend me to fill their vacancies. So, after Brenda and I discussed our options, it became clear that we were going back to Memphis. I was excited about the possibilities!

The next morning, I informed Dr. Gavin of my decision. He wished us well, and asked that I stay in touch. I agreed. The next several weeks passed quickly as there was much to do: sell the house, find housing in Memphis, arrange for our possessions to be sent, and arrange travel with two toddlers. Brenda and I decided the best strategy was for her and the kids to return to Birmingham for the moment. At the last minute, I decided to drive back to Birmingham with them. I had recently received my detachment orders from San Diego and was scheduled to report for duty at Millington Naval Hospital on July 28, 1981. I used my accumulated vacation days to detach early from San Diego. The four of us started the car journey back to Birmingham, finding it a challenge to keep Courtney and Van comfortable. I decided that a dose of Benadryl for each of them would help accomplish this, and it worked. They slept most of the day, allowing me to concentrate on driving. We all arrived safely in Birmingham in three days, and then promptly drove to Memphis to house-hunt. Prior to leaving San Diego, Brenda had arranged for a real estate agent in Memphis to assist us. We managed to find a four-bedroom, two-bath home near Bartlett, Tennessee, conveniently located near Millington, but also close to amenities that Brenda and the kids would need, including day care, kindergarten, and shopping. We decided to purchase the house, assuming ours in San Diego would sell promptly.

The house was located in a middle-class neighborhood on a cul-de-sac, especially appealing as a safety feature for our kids. Brenda and I decided to take early possession so we could be there when our furniture arrived. Prior to leaving Memphis I decided to visit my new duty station in Millington and meet the current radiologists there. The minute I walked in to the radiology department, jaws dropped. Then, red faces started to appear. I was quickly directed to the radiologists' office where only one of them was present. Dr. Keenan was seated, busy interpreting radiographs. I said, "Hi, how are you? My name is Dr. Ellis." I had extended my hand to shake his hand. He looked at my hand, then stood in front of me and refused to shake my hand. His face reddened, then he quickly launched into what my duties would be. No more than three minutes passed; then, he sat down, turned his back to me, and began working.

I was numb but decided to ask one more question, "Where is the other radiologist?"

Dr. Keenan replied, "Dr. Parr's moonlighting in Memphis."

"What is the moonlighting situation here?"

Huffily, he snapped, "You can forget about that! There is none for you!"

I turned to leave, highly disappointed and angry. Not only was I angry at the narrow-minded people I had encountered, but I was also angry at myself for being so trusting, so naïve. I knew instantly that I had made a huge mistake relocating here. Luckily, my can-do spirit took over and convinced me to give it a try. I suppressed my anger and moved on.

The flight back to San Diego was heartbreaking for me. I kept hearing the many voices of individuals in San Diego who were surprised that I would give up the benefits of living there to move to Memphis. After all, I had turned down a coveted position at the Navy's flagship hospital. I recalled attending a social gathering of prominent African American physicians in private practice in San Diego several months earlier. I had met several of them while moonlighting at a private radiology practice in San Diego. They were extremely supportive and encouraged me to stay in San Diego. These physicians were sure that I would be awarded a hospital contract for radiology services in San Diego. Further, they offered their support by promising to refer patients to me. At the time, this all sounded too good to be true, so I was cautious. Physician incomes were lower in San Diego because of a surplus, and the incidence of malpractice lawsuits was also much higher than in Tennessee. Malpractice insurance premiums were considerably higher than those in Memphis. Lastly, hedonism and paganism seemed to be the norm instead of the traditional family values I believed in. If I wanted my marriage to survive, Brenda and I needed to be near family and friends in a traditional, supportive environment. That said, the reception I had received at Millington Naval Hospital smelled of racism. I kept telling myself that maybe I could make a difference in people's perceptions and attitudes by the way I lived, the way I practiced medicine, and the way I maintained a solid family life. I reasoned that it was work that needed to be done, and I would do my part, God willing. I rededicated my life to my mission.

Brenda and I had listed our San Diego home with a real estate agent prior to the trip back to Memphis. He had good news. Our home had three offers at the asking price of $90,000 after being listed for two days! One of the offers was all cash! Of course, I elected to take that offer. The buyer wanted immediate possession, so I arranged for the movers to expedite the move to Memphis, planning to return to Memphis before they arrived. I had just enough time to bid friends farewell, including Dr. Goforth and his wife, Phyllis. Dr. Gavin had just retired with twenty years of military service and was headed back to Seattle for private practice. I thanked him for his unwavering support. He wished me Godspeed in my future endeavors, and offered his prayers for what he knew I would face in Memphis.

Early, before sunrise, I started my journey back to the mid-South, and to Memphis to complete my mission. As my car crested the San Jacinto mountain range, the rising sun appeared on the horizon, the start of a new day, and for me a new beginning.

CHAPTER 6

Private Practice

B renda, Courtney, Van, and I settled into our new home in Memphis, and I reported for duty as the new radiologist at Millington Naval Hospital. I met with the commanding officer of the hospital, Captain Peters, and his staff, who briefed me on my responsibilities as chairman of the radiology department. I inquired about the second radiologist who was to report for duty with me. Another surprise—he would not arrive until the first part of January! *Damn*, I thought to myself, *my worst fear had come to pass; I'll be solo for the next six months!*

Once this meeting concluded, I was escorted to my office in the radiology department. My office already had my name on the door with an addition: Chief of Radiology. One of the great equalizers in the military was rank. I had been recently promoted to lieutenant commander. I met with my radiology personnel under my command and was pleased with the level of respect I received. All of the personnel seemed well trained. I was fortunate to have a senior Navy chief who ran the department like a well-oiled machine. After the meeting, the chief pulled me aside and said, "It appears that the previous radiologists left you a present." He took me into my office and introduced me to the many stacks of uninterrupted radiographs left for me by my predecessors. *Why am I surprised?*

I turned to the chief and said, "Well, it appears that I am going to be very busy."

He responded, "Please sit down, sir. There is more to talk about." I sat, and he continued, "Our work load in radiology has significantly increased such that we need at least four to five additional technologists. The workload for the radiologists is approaching the need for three radiologists. I'm afraid that you're going to be so busy that you may burn out. The command here also wants us to read and perform as many radiology studies as possible and to limit the number of radiology studies referred to civilian radiology departments in the area. The command wants us to start performing ultrasound and mammography in the radiology department rather than sending these exams to civilian practices. In the past, over one hundred radiology exams performed each day at the various satellite clinics were sent to civilian practices for interpretation. We have been asked to interpret these studies here instead. Sir, how do they expect you to do all of this work by yourself?"

I began to get that sinking feeling that I was going to fail. Outwardly, I tried to appear enthusiastic. I stood up from my seat, looked the chief in the eyes, and announced, "Chief, all of us will work hard to accomplish our mission. I want it understood that I will work as hard, or even harder, than anyone in the department. I ask for everyone's cooperation, dedication, and support."

The chief responded, "Yes sir, we will all work together and get this done! Sir, thank you for your support. We have never had that before from a radiologist." The chief left my office and I began to work on the many stacks of uninterpreted radiology studies. I worked hard until 7:30 that evening, but I still got home in time to read bedtime stories to Courtney and Van.

The next day started smoothly, but by midday all hell had broken loose. Several physicians had demanded interpretations on radiology studies performed over two weeks ago. The dictated radiology reports had not reached the ordering physicians. I promptly interpreted their examinations and personally reviewed these studies with the referring doctors in the department. One major complaint was that no one seemed to get a dictated radiology report back after their patients underwent the tests. Few radiology reports reached the patient's medical record. The department was constantly bombarded with requests for interpretations. I thought to myself, *I have transferred myself from San Diego into a real mess*! My first challenge was to reestablish a good reputation and respect for radiology and radiologists. Before I arrived, it was common for the referring physicians to interpret their own radiology studies, since they never got back a report, or the report arrived more than two weeks after the patient had been seen. I was appalled by this, as I felt it greatly affected the credibility of the department. I was determined to remedy this; failure was unacceptable. I diligently worked long, hard days to meet or exceed expectations. I started my day by 7 a.m., and usually left by 7 p.m., Monday through Friday, usually working through the lunch hour. To attempt to catch up on all of the backlogged studies, I even worked many Saturday mornings. I had the technologists track dictated radiology reports to discover the reason behind the delayed reports or the disappearance of radiology reports. One morning, three months later, the lead petty officer knocked on my office door and entered breathing heavily. "Doc, guess what?"

I replied, "What's wrong?"

He answered, "Doc, we found all the missing radiology reports!"

"Where were they?"

"You'll never believe it!" It seems the elevator had malfunctioned that morning, the bottom edge of the elevator stopping at least six inches above the floor level on the ground floor. When the workmen entered the elevator shaft to repair the problem, they discovered thousands of radiology reports!" The petty officer continued, "Man, the commanding officer of the hospital is pissed! I heard that the individuals responsible are going to be court-martialed!"

The individual responsible for this fiasco was quickly identified and immediately discharged from the Navy. Within one week of the elevator incident, radiology reports were reaching the referring physicians and medical records within twenty-four to forty-eight hours. The radiology department received special recognition from the commanding officer of the hospital for this significant improvement in service, which added significantly to the improvement of patient management and care.

My home was my refuge from the stress of managing a busy radiology service with more than enough work for two radiologists. Brenda and I seemed to be more tolerant of and respectful to each other. Courtney and Van always made me feel welcome and special. I was busy and involved with them and their activities. One of our special activities was enjoying the swimming pool. It was summertime, and summertime in Memphis is hot! Once I arrived home, everyone except Brenda jumped into the swimming pool to cool off and play Marco Polo or pool tag. They grew so fast; by the end of the summer, I could not catch them anymore when we played pool tag. I felt that I was extremely blessed to witness my children develop. I also felt blessed to be in the neighborhood I lived in. The neighborhood was secluded by large mature trees, shrubs, and a fence that dampened traffic noise. Our neighbors were friendly; several families had children of similar age to Courtney and Van. All the children played together, but the adults never socialized with us, nor we with them. We were fortunate to have friends from medical school with children for Courtney and Van to play with also. Brenda and I thought it would be a good idea to invite the radiology department over for a social gathering as our way of thanking them for their hard work in an understaffed department. We also felt that this was a way for us to reach out to get to know some of our staff. We expected a small number of individuals to attend but were stunned by the overwhelming response: nearly the entire department attended this gathering at our home. We all had a great time swimming, eating, and getting to know each other better. Afterward, the entire department solidly supported me in my efforts to improve the department.

Brenda's health was never an issue until after the birth of Van. Prior to leaving San Diego, she had developed persistent right knee pain. I took her to a Navy orthopedic surgeon for evaluation. His diagnosis was that Brenda had a form of bursitis. He started her on anti-inflammatory therapy, which seemed to alleviate her symptoms, but they returned six months after arriving in Memphis. This time, she was experiencing some weakness in her right leg as well. I was alarmed and worried, asking myself, *Why would a young, apparently healthy woman develop puzzling leg pain and weakness?* I decided to get her an appointment at Campbell's clinic, a highly regarded orthopedic practice. She was quickly evaluated and the examining physician thought that her right leg weakness was probably secondary to a herniated disc in her lower lumbar spine. I was severely chastised by the orthopedic surgeon for not getting Brenda in for medical help sooner. We were referred to a well-known neurology clinic. After this evaluation, Brenda received a myelogram showing a rather small defect, which puzzled me. I informed both the orthopedic and neurosurgery physicians involved in her care that I had reservations about their diagnosis. I wondered if something more sinister was occurring; I was worried about multiple sclerosis, also known as MS. In 1981, this was a difficult diagnosis to make, and I prayed that I was wrong. Multiple sclerosis was a terrible disease, a devastating and debilitating illness, often affecting women in their prime.

The neurosurgeon thought that he should operate because the myelogram was abnormal. The surgery went well, but I was never told what the surgeon found; and, sadly, there was no improvement of Brenda's symptoms. She did physical therapy for two months without improvement. In fact, I thought she was weaker, so I had her re-examined by a very respected neurologist, Dr. Patrick O'Kane. His examination confirmed that she was weaker. He too felt that the small defect seen on the myelogram could not explain her symptoms and recommended more testing including an EEG, EBR testing, and a spinal tap to collect spinal fluid for analysis. All of these tests were abnormal and consistent with a demyelinating process. Brenda and I finally had an answer for her symptoms: MS. I fully understood the ramifications of this disease: suffering increasing pain, weakness, and dependency on others as the disease progressed. That night I prayed to God to grant our family time to enjoy each other and to slow the progress of Brenda's disease.

One month after her diagnosis was made, Brenda experienced her first MS attack. She developed acute lower extremity weakness and extreme difficulty with balance and walking. Dr. O'Kane hospitalized her and discussed therapy options. There were no drugs available to stop the progress of the disease then. The therapy of choice was high dose-steroids, although some chemotherapy compounds were being tested as a treatment option. Brenda and I chose steroid treatment. She responded well, regaining the ability to walk with the assistance of a walker. All of us were elated that she could walk again! We all thanked God. We went on with our lives; but, secretly, I wondered how much time we would have before the next MS attack.

Nationally, the economy was shaken by double-digit inflation and little to no growth, giving birth to the term "stagflation." Our newly elected president, Ronald Reagan, promised economic recovery and growth by lowering taxes and promoting the principle of trickle-down economics as the solution for the sick economy. Reagan's election to the presidency received mixed reactions in the African American community. There was the fear that little if any benefit would reach common working people or the poor. Furthermore, massive cuts in social programs were feared necessary to pay for the tax cuts. Reagan's conservative values did appeal to the majority of Americans, including significant numbers in the black community. The African Americans I knew during my childhood and currently were decent, hard-working, family oriented, and spiritual. I remembered when I was on welfare and living with my uncle, how I yearned to get off of welfare, and work to become a taxpaying citizen; this was the desire of others I knew on welfare. The individuals I knew aspired to achieve, to make their lives and their children's lives better through hard work, education, and decency. Many Americans I knew felt patronized by the Democrats, while Republicans like Jack Kemp supported small business development and entrepreneurship in the black community. The Republican Party seemed to offer real hope and not handouts. For many African Americans, now was the time to return to the party of Abraham Lincoln. I was one of them; I favored not only Reagan's economic policies, but also his belief in a strong military. In fact, the Americans held hostage in Iran were released immediately following his inauguration.

The loss of moonlighting income I was expecting upon my arrival back in Memphis hurt my family financially. Brenda's health stabilized for the remainder of 1982, but I badly needed to earn extra money to pay for the extras we needed such as improving the handicapped accessibility of our home and cars. There were devices one could purchase to modify cars so that a handicapped individual could continue to drive. I also needed extra money to help pay for day care for Courtney and Van so that Brenda could get time for additional rest and physical therapy. Moonlighting was the best option.

Every practice that offered moonlighting opportunities was interested in me until I appeared in person for the interview. One evening, after the usual long day at the hospital, I discovered an advertisement in one of my radiology journals by a *locum tenens* company looking for radiologists. I decided to contact them and received an immediate response once they had received my credentials. There was a need for coverage for a radiology practice in Spencer, Iowa. The company made all the necessary arrangements, including temporary licensure, travel, and lodging. I was excited that I was going to see a part of America that I never thought I would. I spoke several times with the radiologist whose practice I would be covering, Dr. Grice. He was happy to get coverage so that he could take a well-deserved vacation. I was happy to finally get the opportunity to earn the extra money I needed for my family. Of course, I could not leave for this assignment until the second radiologist reported for duty at the Naval Hospital, and it was near the middle of January before that happened.

I decided to accept an assignment near the end of March to allow the new radiologist to adapt. Brenda felt strong enough to manage at home during my absence. She was happy that I found the work, but sad that I had to travel to Iowa for it. The weekend before the last week of March I began the journey to Spencer. The flight was memorable indeed. There was routine jet service between Memphis and Des Moines, although travel between Des Moines and Spencer was via propeller plane. I was okay with that until I saw the plane. It was a Piper Cub plane with seating for the pilot and one passenger. I was terrified at first, but then the adventurer and inquisitive little boy part of me took over. I talked myself into thinking that this would be fun! I entered the plane with my single bag of luggage. The pilot introduced himself. "Hello young man, I'm Mike." (Mike appeared to be approximately fifty years old.) "As soon as you're ready we can depart for Spencer. The weather is great, so I don't anticipate any problems or significant turbulence."

I replied, "Hello, Mike. This is my first trip in such a small plane. I am a bit anxious." (I started to tremble slightly as I spoke.)

Mike replied, "Now don't you worry young man. I have been flying for twenty-five years; you are in good hands." I turned to glance back and inspected the rear of the plane's cabin and spotted a rather large bottle of Jack Daniels!

I inquired, "What's the big bottle of liquor for?"

He laughed. "Oh, for the folks who need to calm their nerves, especially if the flying gets a little rough." I panicked. I was about to ask him to let me out when he turned his head, gunned the engine and started the drive down the runway.

We were airborne in no time at all. I closed my eyes, swallowed hard and tried to relax. After a few minutes I decided to open my eyes and was stunned by the beauty I was surrounded by! I felt that I was literally floating along, occasionally passing through small clouds. The sky was crystal blue, the sun appeared as a bright fireball that I could only glance at, as I did not have sunglasses.

Mike said, "What's your name?"

"James," I replied.

"And what brings you to this part of the country?"

"I am headed to Spencer to cover a medical practice for one week while the doctor there takes a vacation."

Mike nodded. "So you must be a doctor?"

"Yes, I am."

"I am sure you had to go to school a long time. You don't appear to be that old. If I may ask, how old are you?"

"I just had my thirty-first birthday a month ago, in February."

"Wow," he exclaimed. "I thought you were no more than twenty-two or twenty-three!"

I replied, "Thank you, sir. I try to take care of myself. I believe that if doctors are healthy, their patients tend to be more compliant with guidelines for maintaining their own health."

Mike laughed, "James, that makes perfectly good sense."

Suddenly the plane quickly lost altitude. It happened so quickly, I barely had a chance to respond. I screamed out, "Shit! I am going to die!"

Mike responded, "Calm down, James, everything is under control." I slowly opened my eyes to look around, ever so slightly easing my death grip on the armrests. The plane was flying smoothly.

"I'm sorry, Mike," I said. "I thought I was going to die!"

He said, "James, you're flying with one of the best. I have never crashed a plane. I learned how to fly in the Air Force and flew commercial airlines after my military service. Flying is in my blood." I had beads of sweat on my forehead, but Mike seemed unmoved and unshaken, resolute, and stable. He continued, "If you think you needed it, please help yourself to the Jack Daniels bottle. That is what it's there for."

I shook my head. "Thanks, but I think I'm going to be okay." We were starting to slowly descend. There were numerous farms all around, as far as the eye could see, sectioned into perfect squares, appearing as sections of a vast tapestry or quilt. As we approached the airport to land, I could see that the endless green carpet represented vast cornfields! I breathed a sigh of relief as the plane landed. Happy to have my feet touch the ground, I hurried to grab my bag and headed into the very tiny airport terminal. I turned briefly to wave goodbye to Mike.

Dr. Grice was there to meet me. "You must be Dr. Ellis," he said, holding out his hand.

I shook it and said, "Yes sir I am. Pleased to meet you. Thank you for allowing me to cover your practice."

Dr. Grice replied, "I am honored to have you cover my practice. You are well-trained and you come highly recommended. Let me take you to your hotel so that you can get comfortable and get some rest. You don't mind if we make a brief detour to the hospital, do you?" Dr. Grice's car was a brand-new silver Buick Riviera, with a female driver I assumed to be his wife, but he said, "Dr. Ellis, I would like for you to meet my secretary, Ms. Janssen."

I responded, "Pleased to meet you ma'am."

Ms. Janssen said, "Pleased to meet you also, Dr. Ellis. Welcome to Spencer. I am Dr. Grice's transcriptionist and chauffeur."

She drove on, and Dr. Grice gave me some more information. "I cover three hospitals: the main hospital here in Spencer, another small hospital located in Storm Lake, and a third hospital located five miles south of Spencer. I find that I am much more efficient by providing my own transcription service, so that my reports are ready to be signed once I'm ready to leave the hospital. I am also studying for my law degree, so I use the time to study while Ms. Janssen drives between hospitals."

"You are really organized," I replied.

Dr. Grice smiled. "Well, let's drive to the Spencer hospital to go over a few details, and then we'll get you to the hotel." Dr. Grice gave me a quick tour of the radiology department. Next, I was taken to a small hotel and shown to my room. I quickly fell asleep after talking with Brenda, Courtney, and Van.

Dr. Grice's secretary arrived at the hotel by six o'clock to take me to the Spencer hospital to begin my day. I worked hard, and by 9 a.m., my work was completed and my radiology reports signed. Dr. Grice's secretary then informed me that the next hospital on our schedule was about a thirty- to forty-minute drive south to a town called Storm Lake. She gave me the keys to the car and directions to the hospital and off I went. At approximately 1:30, I left the second hospital, returned to the main hospital in Spencer, interpreted more radiology studies, signed reports, and then left to drive to the third hospital located in a town called Spirit Lake. By 4:30 I was back at the Spencer hospital to finish the day. I ate dinner around 6:30 and was in bed two hours later, falling fast asleep.

The entire week went well. The staff and physicians were

all cordial and most helpful. Everyone, I mean everyone, smiled here! Patients were respectful. One elderly lady promised to bake a cake for me if I came back. I was also invited to come back by the staff and physicians at all three hospitals. I arrived home by Saturday afternoon, tired but pleased with the experience. Monday morning Dr. Grice called to thank me for covering his practice. He wanted me to commit to additional coverage for his practice in the future. Of course, I agreed. My check from the locum tenens company arrived on Wednesday. Brenda and I were most pleased, and yes, she too agreed to let me accept future assignments to Dr. Grice's practice in Iowa.

When I returned home, I got to work some more with the new radiologist. Dr. Eagleton was the long-awaited second radiologist who reported for duty at Naval Hospital Millington. Dr. Eagleton had just completed her radiology residency at Presbyterian Hospital in Memphis. She, like me, was the recipient of a Navy scholarship for medical school. She had chosen to serve her obligated military service at Millington because of the proximity to her hometown, Paris, Tennessee. She was inexperienced, but willing to learn. I was happy to have help and not face such a backlog of work during my absence. Since the department was functioning smoothly, I decided to return to Spencer to cover Dr. Grice's practice near the end of May.

Spring was in full-bloom in Iowa. Spencer was alive with flowers, brilliantly green grass, and budding trees. The sky was a crisp light blue, the air was full of the fragrance of honeysuckle. A symphony of melodious chirps emanating from flying birds, an occasional butterfly floating by, gave me the feeling of being home in my Richmond backyard as a child. I felt wanted, needed, and respected here in Spencer. I was not only greeted with smiles but also now acknowledged by name: "Hi, Dr. Ellis, welcome back!" The level of approval I felt was nourishing for my psyche, rivaling the nourishing approval I got from the many pats on my head and shoulders by Mrs. Epps and other mentors. The thought even occurred to me, *Maybe I should consider moving to Iowa.* However, that thought was quickly erased on Friday morning, my last day to cover the practice. I awoke to a record snowfall event! The weather up to this point had been perfect: temperatures in the sixties, with plenty of sunshine. Now, the wind was blowing and there was at least a foot of snow on the ground! I made it to the main hospital because the road crews were out in force clearing the roads, but the roads outside Spencer were closed. I received an emergency call from the surgeon at the Storm Lake Hospital. He needed me to help him with a very sick patient. I prayed, and started the drive to the hospital. The road was covered with at least eight to twelve inches of snow. The only boundaries I could make out were telephone poles and fences. The trip usually took thirty minutes. I reached the hospital after a nerve-wracking one-and-a-half hours!

I immediately proceeded to radiology where the surgeon and his very ill patient were. The technician had just completed an abdominal radiograph that I reviewed with the surgeon. The patient was very large, which limited the clarity of the radiograph, but no intestinal gas was present. Clinically, the surgeon was considering the possibility of an ileus, although small bowel obstruction was a possibility. The surgeon wanted to know if I could perform and interpret ultrasound. I replied affirmatively. The tech presented me with a small portable ultrasound unit that I was unfamiliar with. However, I quickly learned how to operate it and proceeded to scan the patient's abdomen. The images were not the best but were diagnostic, demonstrating the presence of multiple fluid-filled dilated small bowel loops. I also thought that the small bowel walls were abnormally thickened; I thought the ultrasound images were consistent with the presence of a high-grade small bowel obstruction. The surgeon took the patient to surgery immediately.

Later that evening, I received a call from the surgeon, thanking me for my help. He informed me that the patient had a significant small bowel obstruction, and was doing well after surgery. He asked me to come back soon or to consider relocating to the area. I was flattered, and thanked him for his comments. The next morning, I traveled back to Memphis, completely satisfied and thoroughly convinced that I had chosen the right profession to accomplish my dream of contributing to society for the betterment of mankind. I was grateful for the opportunity that Dr. Grice and the people of Iowa had given me.

It was fall, 1982. My obligated military service would end in July 1983. I needed to determine if I wanted to reenlist for additional military duty, with a definite possibility of returning to San Diego, staying in Memphis, relocating to Iowa (although the spring snow event I had experienced there made this location less desirable), or perhaps to the East Coast. The Navy wanted me reenlist. The commanding officer at Millington assured me that I would be promoted to the rank of commander soon. He further stated that I should also obtain the rank of captain (colonel) and that I had the potential to obtain flag rank (admiral). However, I wanted the best opportunity for my family, and decided that private practice was the way to obtain this. I wanted Brenda to have the best medical care possible for her multiple sclerosis. I wanted to be able to afford to send Courtney and Van to the college of their choice. I checked the American College of Radiology listings for private practice opportunities, and found two opportunities of interest to me.

The first private practice opportunity was located in a small suburb outside of Indianapolis, Indiana. The senior and founding partner was retiring. The practice of five radiologists covered three hospitals located within fifteen minutes of each other. I was invited to look at the practice, and of course the five partners and their families would get to meet me. I spent one full day getting to know the partners and the practice environment. Everyone was cordial; the neighborhoods were sound—schools, public and private, were considered excellent. All of the partners expressed a strong interest in me, stating that the position was mine if I wanted it. I met with the retiring partner who was also the founder of this group to discuss financial matters. He also stated that he wanted to hire me. The monetary offer he gave me seemed fair. I was excited and could not wait to inform Brenda that we would be moving to Indianapolis! I was told to give the group three days to finalize details of the offer and to call back. I returned home, discussed the offer with Brenda, and started making plans to move.

The three days passed slowly. I made the phone call expecting good news, but was shocked by what I heard. I was told that while I was the best candidate for the group, there were a couple of referring doctors, both surgeons, who objected to working with me. I was told that they would make life difficult for me. They also threatened to refer their patients to competing radiology groups if I was hired. I was told that the surgeon who most vehemently opposed me was Chinese! I was so disheartened that I contemplated not exploring any other opportunities. Brenda and I talked, and I decided to try looking at the second practice opportunity located in Humboldt, Tennessee, a small town located approximately one hour cast of Memphis. An expanding hospital was searching for a radiologist to develop a hospital practice there. I sent them my CV and received a phone call from the hospital administrator. He invited Brenda and me to come visit. During our phone conversation, he offered me the practice after evaluating my CV and experience. I was invited to Humboldt to sign an agreement if I felt comfortable, or take a contract with me to ponder and sign if I agreed to accept the offer. The administrator thought that with my expertise, I could develop a very lucrative practice, from which the hospital would benefit as well. Any caution flags raised by the too good to be true feeling I began to experience were completely allayed when he said, "Look, Dr. Ellis, you are a native Tennesseean, highly educated, and we need you here. I have been authorized by the hospital board to guarantee your income for five years! I need to meet with you to determine what baseline salary is acceptable to you. Of course, if you collect more than the minimum, you keep it. We strongly anticipate that you will always exceed the guaranteed income level every year. Please come, bring your wife, and pick out a nice home. We will pay for moving expenses. I and others here look forward to meeting you!"

Brenda and I were elated! We arrived in Humboldt and proceeded directly to the hospital. We were fifteen minutes early so the secretary seated us in the administrator's office. He arrived in less than five minutes. As he entered the office, a bewildered, stunned look overtook his facial expression as he inquired, "Are you Dr. Ellis?"

"Yes," I replied. I extended my hand to shake his hand but he refused.

He then inquired, "Are you sure?"

"Yes, I really am sure," I said.

His face quickly turned from very pale to bright red. He quickly regained his composure, and responded apologetically, "Dr. and Mrs. Ellis, please forgive me." He paused, then added, "We have a problem—er, well, we'll talk while I give you a quick tour of our city."

After some more hemming and hawing he finally managed to say, "I am so sorry. Look, I didn't know that you were black, Dr. Ellis. That is a problem because there are physicians on our staff who would make life extremely difficult for you. They would not support your practice, I am sure. Please understand that this area is still very conservative and well, I"— again that pause—"I mean, *we* are not used to seeing black people as educated and as talented as you are." Brenda and I looked at each other, held hands, stood, and thanked him for his time before walking out to our car. We sat there for a brief period in silence. Our eyes welled up with tears as we looked at each other. As I looked at Brenda, I felt a surge of emotions that I saw mirrored in her eyes: the trail of tears shed by our ancestors, those who had passed along this same journey before. We wondered how much longer would future generations have opportunity's door closed in their face just because we were black.

My greatest joy was my family—Courtney, Van, Brenda, and the refuge my home provided. The outcome of the recent Humboldt visit underscored the importance of a solid family unit, especially during difficult times. No matter how difficult the outside world was, there was always a joy and unconditional love that family provided. Courtney and Van always greeted me with a cheerful chant, "Yay, it's Daddy! Yay, yay for Daddy!" This was followed by each of them grabbing one of my legs and hugging it. I felt like a kid whenever I spent time with them. We played hide-and-seek, football, racing, and of course swimming in the pool. Courtney and Van were excellent swimmers. Brenda did not care to swim, but enjoyed watching the kids and me swim and play. We also enjoyed reading books. I made sure that every night I read to them. Courtney and Van never seem to tire of hearing me read some of their favorite stories over and over. I entertained them by imitating certain characters such as the Cat in the Hat, Thing One and Thing Two, and other characters especially from the *Sweet Pickles* book series. Each night, we prayed together before retiring to bed.

Courtney and Van had wonderful playmates in the neighborhood and others that they befriended in day care, and later in kindergarten and elementary school. Our kids loved all things pizza, especially at Chuck E. Cheese, where we all spent many fun times. Our kids were happy and healthy. They also benefited from having a tight-knit family. The close proximity of Birmingham was therapeutic for Brenda as members of her family came to visit us often. Occasionally, Mom and other members of my family visited also. Because of all this, Brenda and I decided to stay in Memphis. I could continue to do locums work with a locum tenens company until I found that perfect practice opportunity.

Dr. Eagleton inquired about my job search. I told her about the visit to Humboldt, and the lack of moonlighting work locally. She chuckled, looked me in the eye, and said, "You know where you are, don't you, Jim? This is the South; you will never get a private practice opportunity here. What are you going to do when a patient calls you a nigger and spits in your face?" I blinked, not believing what I just heard—but it resonated with me. This was harsh reality; professionally, I was treated as a second-class citizen once I left the naval base. Something within me strongly resisted accepting the status quo; I knew this was the way it is, but not the way it should be.

I looked at Dr. Eagleton and spoke firmly but calmly. "With all that is in me, I will do my part to make it the way it should be. I will be relentless; I won't rest until the seeds of fairness and opportunity have taken root in radiology in this area." Saying nothing else, we both turned and went back to work. The day ended and we went our separate ways silently.

Since I had committed to staying in Memphis, I decided to enhance my professional skill set by completing a fellowship in a subspecialty area of radiology. Significant technical advances were occurring in MR imaging, ultrasound, and CT. Expert interpretation of these images by radiologists was mandatory. Radiology groups looking to add additional partners favored candidates who were trained in a subspecialty area. I approached the chairman of the University of Tennessee radiology department with my request for fellowship training in body imaging, which would include gaining expertise in all three of the aforementioned areas. I was invited to a dinner meeting with Dr. Guerra, the department chairman, and Dr. Tomlin. After trading pleasantries, they made the financial offer, much below my current Navy salary. Dr. Guerra reassured me that I could earn supplemental income to help match my Navy income. I decided to accept the fellowship, to begin near the end of July, once my military obligation had been completed. I felt good about this decision for professional reasons; there was also a sense of comfort in returning to my alma mater. I was well received by all, which was slightly surprising to me, but greatly appreciated.

By the end of the year, Dr. Guerra invited me to join the radiology department as a new faculty member once I completed my fellowship. I was honored to accept this offer and felt blessed to remain in Memphis, hoping that one day a private practice opportunity would come my way. Still, even if that never happened, I was satisfied where I was. I was a professor of radiology at a major medical school and medical center, with the respect of my peers as well as those I taught and trained. I attended at least two major continuing medical education meetings a year in radiology, which provided a chance for me to network with radiologists in other practice locations nationwide. I met several African American radiologists, and I discovered that we were a rarity. In 1984, the total number of radiologists in the United States was approximately twenty-five thousand. Less than 1 percent were African American! The vast majority practiced in the large cities on the coasts, almost always affiliated with the teaching hospitals of university medical schools. Rarely did I meet any African American radiologists who were in private practice. Their stories reflected my experiences of being shunned by private practices fearful of adding an African American to their practice lest they lose income when prejudiced doctors chose to refer their patients to other radiology practices. It was sobering to realize that after years of fighting this type of discrimination, many years after the passage of civil rights legislation, the old Jim Crow practices regarding professional employment in the South and many other locations across America was still the law of the land. It was shocking to me that extremely well-educated professionals such as doctors practiced and supported this type of discrimination. I was well-educated, attended one of the best prep schools in America, a highly regarded engineering college, and a respectable medical school. I had received sound training as a doctor and a specialist in radiology. I was board certified in my specialty. I was a good doctor by all criteria, yet the private practice door remained closed.

I tried hard to accept the reality I lived in; yet no matter how hard I tried, my intense feelings of anger and resentment could not be pacified by acceptance alone. I did the only thing I knew how to do; I buried these feelings deep within my psyche, put on a happy face, and moved on.

Brenda's health began to deteriorate again during the winter of 1984. She experienced a massive MS attack, which completely paralyzed her lower extremities. Again, she was hospitalized and treated with steroids. Miraculously, the treatment worked well enough that she was able to walk out of the hospital. I thanked God! Brenda walked with a cane, and she was able to continue driving, perform errands, transport Courtney and Van to their various activities, including childcare. Privately, I worried and fretted about my family's future and Brenda's health, for I knew what multiple sclerosis would do. The next attack could change our lives radically and quickly; it was more than likely that ten years on she would become bedridden. My plan was to take a family vacation every year and travel to a special place. Our very first vacation was to Opryland in Nashville, Tennessee. In 1985, we traveled to St. Louis, Missouri, and enjoyed the many tourist attractions there. Seeing the Gateway Arch up close and personal was thrilling; it would've been spectacular to ride to the top of the Arch, but the lines were too long, and it was very hot. Next, we traveled to San Diego, staying at the Intercontinental Hotel. It was wonderful to be reunited with Brenda's brother Johnny and his wife, who made a special trip to San Diego and offered to take Courtney and Van to Disneyland in Los Angeles. Brenda and I thought it was a great idea; we would drive up to Los Angeles the next day to pick them up. Brenda and I enjoyed a wonderful evening together, and then we drove to Los Angeles the next morning to pick up the kids. When we arrived, we noticed a look of tension in the faces of Johnny and his wife. They informed us that Van had wandered away while at Disneyland! Fortunately, he was located two hours later on the premises. They were still shaken by how quickly he disappeared, thinking that he had been kidnapped! I became more vigilant about the kids' whereabouts and safety after this incident. I decided that we would all stick together on any future vacations.

We traveled together to Gatlinburg and Dolly Land in east Tennessee. Courtney and Van wanted to go back to Disneyland, so I decided to schedule a trip to Disney World in Orlando, since it was less stressful for Brenda to travel shorter distances. The trip to Disney World was for six days and five nights and we had a ball. Somehow a timeshare company got our name and address and offered us free lodging for our next trip to Disney World. Of course, they expected us to purchase a timeshare week for future vacations to Disney World. We tried it out, and it was fabulous. The timeshare accommodations and amenities were superb. Since we enjoyed traveling to Orlando and Disney World, Brenda and I decided to purchase a timeshare week with this organization. We vacationed in Orlando every year from the mid-80s to early '90s. Our kids grew up at Disney World and Universal Studios. Also, the theme parks and the entire city of Orlando were extremely sensitive to the needs of handicapped and special-needs vacationers. Brenda and I wished that the rest of the world would take more interest in accommodating the handicapped vacationer.

By 1993, we all were somewhat bored with the annual trips to Orlando. I investigated other options for vacation. We tried swapping our timeshare week for an alternative vacation location, but were not satisfied with the accommodations we received. Then, I read about cruising. There were many advantages such as handicapped accessible quarters, great food and entertainment, as well as travel to multiple desirable locations during the cruise trip. We accumulated a multitude of lifetime memories as well as pictures during these cruise vacations. At the end of our last cruise vacation in 1996, Brenda was notably weaker. She indicated that this was the last cruise for her, and therefore for all of us.

Courtney and Van seemed to transform rapidly from children to teenagers. Courtney excelled academically, graduating as the salutatorian of her St. Mary's class in 1996. Van, who is highly intelligent, succumbed to peer pressure and played the dumb-down game. He was extremely sociable and enjoyed great popularity during his high school years. Van aspired to become an actor and performed in several plays locally. He landed the stand-in role for the lead actor in the movie *Hustle and Flow*. Courtney graduated from Harvard and obtained her law degree from Vanderbilt University in Nashville. Brenda and I are extremely proud of the adults Courtney and Van have become.

In 1985, I accepted an opportunity with a managed care organization in Memphis. I left the university and became the sole radiologist for a multispecialty group. I soon realized that I had gotten myself into another undesirable situation. I sincerely wanted this opportunity to develop into a large radiology practice that produced significant income for the entire group, but I had many enemies within the group. I was told that there was a lot of fear of me developing my own radiology empire. But that attitude was self-fulfilling; it became crystal clear to me that I needed to control my own destiny, so after three years, I resigned to pursue building my own radiology practice. I successfully secured a civilian contract to provide radiology services for Naval Hospital Millington. There were not enough Navy radiologists, so the radiology department was civilianized. I hired another radiologist to help me on this contract. He offered to take me to lunch as a show of gratitude.

On October 20, 1988, the unthinkable happened. It was a rainy, dreary day. I wanted to drive my Volvo to lunch, but my new partner insisted on driving his car, a subcompact. My only memory is that we were talking and he was about to make a left turn. My next memory was a loud noise that turned out to be the jaws of life cutting the car from around me. Someone said, "Hey, look, he's alive!" I couldn't feel a thing.

I was removed from the wreckage and placed on a flat board. I noticed that my right thigh was especially swollen and began to hurt. My pain became more intense as the ambulance hurried to the nearest emergency room, at North Presbyterian Hospital. I must have lost consciousness, because then I felt someone shaking me, saying, "Jim, can you hear me? How do you feel?" There were several doctors standing over me. Once my vision resolved, there was one face I recognized, that of Dr. Herman Col. Dr. Col and his father had been my supervising staff at the West Tennessee Chest Hospital rotation during medical school. The younger Dr. Col spoke to me again, "Jim, how do you feel?"

I whispered, "What happened?"

Dr. Col said, "You were involved in a serious car accident. I'm glad you're talking. I thought we were going to lose you. Your blood pressure was 70 over 10 but has recovered and is much better since I placed a central line in and started big time fluid replacement. You're probably bleeding internally, so we're going to get a CT scan of your abdomen and pelvis and your right leg."

"My leg?" I started to panic. "What's wrong with my leg?"

"I think your right leg is broken," replied Dr. Col. It was then that I noticed increasing pain in my right thigh. I reached down to touch my right thigh and felt nothing.

"Am I paralyzed?"

"I don't think so, Jim. Let's see what the CT scan shows." I was quickly taken to the radiology department for my scan.

I knew most of the radiology department at North Presbyterian Hospital. During my tour of duty at Naval Hospital Millington, I discovered that many patients were taking their radiology studies from the Navy base for second opinions by civilian radiologists. Usually, these radiologists agreed with my radiology interpretation, although of course there were occasional disagreements.

As I rolled into the radiology department, I thought about one of the more memorable face-to-face discussions that had occurred here. The case involved the wife of a military retiree. She worked at Naval Hospital Millington and received one of the first mammogram examinations offered by my department. The exams were state-of-the-art xeromammograms. I had interpreted her exam as being abnormal, so I recommended a biopsy. As I reviewed her mammogram study with the other radiologists and the surgeon, it became very apparent to me that a decision had already been made; that is, I was being told to change my interpretation to a negative reading because it was wrong. However, I refused to change my interpretation; I did not want to miss an early cancer that would mean a cure if my recommendation was followed. I remember being told that if I was wrong, I should not read mammograms anymore. Two days later, the patient was taken to surgery after a localization procedure was performed; the suspicious area in her breast was removed. The initial frozen section interpretation of the specimen was benign and she was released to go home. However, the final pathology report the next morning showed cancer present—carcinoma in situ, a very early cancer. The patient was treated surgically (mastectomy) and did well. She paid me a personal visit after surgery, hugged and thanked me, and gave me a wonderful homemade pie.

I was snapped back to reality by a voice in the CT scan suite, "Hello, Dr. Ellis, I'll be interpreting your scan. We want to make it as comfortable as possible for you. If you don't have any questions, we will proceed."

I replied, "No questions. Will you let me know what you see once the exam is over?" The radiologist said, "It will be my pleasure."

Once the scanning process was over, the radiologist informed me that my injuries were severe. I had sustained multiple fractures to my pelvis and right femur and had a large pelvic hematoma (blood clot) associated with the pelvic fractures. I was immediately transferred to the intensive care unit for stabilization so that my fractures could be treated surgically. My right leg was elevated and placed in traction to facilitate alignment of the multiple fragments prior to surgery. The orthopedic surgeon, Dr. Harris, stated that he could not perform surgery until my medical condition stabilized.

Next, Dr. Clayton Jonas, a respected and well-known general surgeon, addressed me in a very solemn voice as he looked directly into my eyes. "Jim, you have multiple injuries as well as fractures. You are bleeding slowly internally; therefore, we can't fix your fractures until you're medically stable. I think you currently have an extreme risk for fat embolization because of the extent of your fractures." I knew that fat embolization was often fatal. He went on, "I have consulted a hematologist to help us manage your medical condition, so that surgery on your leg can be performed. Now, your condition is 'guarded to grave.' Let us pray that you can survive these challenges. I assure you we will do everything in our power to help you survive. Do you have any questions?"

"No," I responded. "But I don't feel good. I pray that I won't die; I have so much more I need to do."

The next seventy-two hours would be critical. I looked around me at the numerous life-support lines, tubes, and monitors attached to me. I could not remember the passage of the first twenty-four hours. The nurses told me that I had been in and out of consciousness. Apparently, I had experienced a small fat embolus and survived. However, I was still bleeding internally. Dr. Waxman, a talented hematologist, evaluated my medical condition the following day, and the results were not promising. Dr. Waxman thought that my continued slow bleeding was part of a complex process. All of my blood components, such as platelets, red blood cells, and white cells, were rapidly decreasing. It was thought that I had experienced severe shock at the time of the accident. This process started a chain of events in my body resulting in a rare coagulopathy called disseminating idiopathic coagulopathy. My body's defense system had literally turned on me and was consuming all of my blood components. I would die if the process did not stop or reverse itself. Dr. Waxman had successfully treated this rare but highly fatal condition several times by blood transfusion; if it worked for me, my chances of survival would greatly improve. That evening and throughout the night I received transfusions, getting a total of twelve units. I experienced pain, fever, and restlessness; the nurses said I was delirious most of the night. I remembered reciting the Twenty-Third Psalm several times that night. I must have fallen asleep because when I opened my eyes it was 5 a.m.—I had survived the night. I cried tears of joy and thanked God for giving me another twenty-four hours.

Dr. Clayton was the first physician to check my status. He smiled as he entered my room, greeting me cheerfully, "Well Jim, the blood transfusions appeared to have worked. I am going to upgrade your condition from 'grave' to 'serious and improving.'"

I beamed, "Praise God!" My prayers had been answered. Ten days passed and I grew strong enough to undergo surgical repair of my right femur. The pelvic fractures would heal without surgery. Dr. Harris, the orthopedic surgeon, indicated that the surgical repair of my right femur could result in the shortening of my right leg. Additionally, he thought that it would take several months or longer for me to learn how to walk again. He warned me that I might need the support of a walking cane indefinitely.

Surgery went well. I was stable enough to be moved from intensive care to a standard hospital room for post-op orthopedic patients. During my transfer, I passed by several windows and marveled at my first glimpses of sunlight and the world outside. It was fall, November 1, 1988. The brilliance of the morning sun contrasting with the crystal-blue sky and the multicolored autumn leaves stimulated my senses. I closed my eyes and thanked God again for sparing my life. I thanked him for the many angels sent to my aid and to my family's aid during this life crisis.

I was hospitalized from October 20 to December 16. Angels in the form of friends and strangers kept my family supplied with hot meals and support, for which we'll be forever grateful. I was released from the hospital just in time to celebrate Christmas at home with my family. I was thankful, but also very concerned about my limited physical ability and Brenda's illness. What if she or I fell? Neither one of us could help each other immediately. I decided that we needed to move into a home with the master bedroom downstairs for our safety and convenience. In the interim, I needed to find a way to avoid any such catastrophe. I could not afford to move or build a downstairs bedroom addition, nor could I afford an elevator. I did discover a device called a chairlift, in which a chair sat on a track that was mounted on the stairwell. Fortunately, it was affordable. Brenda and I could now negotiate the stairwell safely.

January 1989 bought good news and seemed to suggest a better year for me. I received a phone call from Dr. Guerra, chairman of the radiology department at the University of Tennessee, Memphis. He invited me to rejoin the radiology staff as an assistant professor of radiology. The position involved teaching and training radiology residents, doing research, and publishing in peer-reviewed radiology journals.

The position included private practice time with the generated income distributed to all members of the radiology department. This offer came on the heels of another phone call from the Department of Defense offering me the radiology contract at Naval Hospital Millington I had recently lost because of the automobile accident. I informed Dr. Guerra of this potential income source; he said if I accepted it, the university's radiology department could become the contract holder. He asked if I could report for work by the end of April. I had been convalescing well at home, but was not comfortable driving yet, and wondered if I was physically and mentally ready to return to work full-time. Brenda and the kids enjoyed having me at home, and I enjoyed being a stay-at-home dad. Yet, I realized that I needed to work to support my family, and I did enjoy practicing my profession. I worked hard to improve my physical mobility with the help of in-home physical therapy. By the beginning of April, I was mobile enough to walk with the assistance of a cane, and had begun to drive. It was time for me to return to work, to the practice of medicine, to the practice of radiology.

I began to search for a new home three months after I started back to work. I was most interested in finding a home or modifying a home to be handicapped-friendly for Brenda. By the early fall, I found just what I needed in a newly completed subdivision in Germantown. Germantown was a suburban city of affluence but with a reputation for smugness and racism, especially directed to African Americans. Still, the house was exactly what we wanted. Most of the living space was on the first floor, as was the master bedroom. The doorways were wide enough to accommodate a wheelchair if necessary. Neighborhood schools were excellent and close by. Shopping was conveniently located. We moved in on December 20, 1989, to spend Christmas in our new home!

There were significant happenings and obstacles to freedom

being removed in the rest of the world. The wall that divided communist East Berlin from democratic West Berlin and Germany had recently come down. The ripple effect spread around the world and appeared to reach even Memphis. This Christmas seemed especially meaningful because of the electricity of freedom, joy, and peace spreading around the world because of the recent decline of communism in Eastern Europe. To me, this event signaled the crumbling and falling apart of the wall separating the races, falling apart piece by piece. It caused me to reflect on the essence of Christmas, its true meaning: the celebration of the birth of our Lord and Savior Jesus Christ, who was born to die for our sins and allow us access to eternal life. I prayed and thanked God for sparing my life in the automobile accident. I thanked him for our beautiful home. Most of all, I thank him for my family, my wife Brenda, my daughter Courtney, and my son Van. Christmas night, after all was quiet and everyone asleep, I pondered my life to this point, remembering my own humble origin and the many Christmases without family, without a father or mother. I was pleased that I was still married to my first and only wife. I was pleased and thankful that I was watching my pride and joy, my children, grow and mature. I felt blessed to be an integral part of their lives in the past, in the present, and in the future. The new year, 1990, was less than a week away.

1990 ushered in one of the coldest winters on record in Memphis. The weather was nasty and I was about to experience some of the cold nastiness of Germantown. My Christmas hope that the spirit of *perestroika* had reached this part of the United States was dashed by a series of disturbing events. We were told by one of the realtors associated with the sale of our home to expect to hear from an organization similar to Welcome Wagon. They provided new families with a wealth of information concerning stores, merchants and services, schools and churches, and other interest clubs or groups. We never received any of this information, but I rationalized that maybe it was an oversight. We enrolled Courtney and Van in the neighborhood middle school. The school bus picked them up near our front door. Out of concern for the welfare of my children, I waited at home until I saw them board the school bus before heading to the hospital. One cold February morning, I observed a young man pushing and shoving my son while my daughter Courtney screamed at him. He was clearly larger and older. Alarmed, I sprinted out of the house and headed to the school bus stop to rescue Van. This boy knocked Van to the ground before I reached him. I was enraged but did not touch the boy. Instead, I pointed my finger in the young man's face and screamed, "You are going to jail!" I quickly assisted my son, and then escorted Courtney and Van back home. I drove them both to school; then I decided to call the police to report the incident. I wanted to press charges, but was encouraged to discuss the matter with the boy's parents, so I did. We all met, and the father stated that the only reason he was speaking with me was because I was ex-military! It did not matter that I was a professional, a physician; he respected the fact that I had served in the United States Navy, as he did. I was momentarily puzzled by this revelation. How had he gotten this kind of information about me? His son apologized for his behavior—reluctantly, it seemed—and Van accepted his apology. *Maybe this is just one of those disagreements between children*, I thought. Several years later, my children and I were reminiscing about previous years and they both informed me that the incident started with racial insults. An isolated incident, that's how most conservatives (myself included) would have explained away events of this nature. However, three months later, a raw egg was thrown against the front wall of my home. I promptly called the police and an officer appeared shortly thereafter. Showing him the fresh egg on the wall, I discovered that apparently several other eggs had landed in the shrubs instead of hitting the wall. I said, "I don't think my neighbors like me, officer. Why else would someone do this?"

He shrugged and said, "Well, Mr. Ellis, it may just be vandalism. You would think such actions would not occur in a well-to-do upper-class neighborhood like this, but unfortunately it does quite frequently. I'm sorry, but there is not much I can do now. Please do call again if this continues to occur."

No further incidents occurred, but the coldness of the past winter seemed to linger into the spring and summer. Neighbors never smiled, often looking down or past us if we happened to walk by them. The traditional handshake was out of the question. This type of behavior was especially poignant in the area churches. Prior to moving to Germantown, we attended a predominantly African American church near midtown in Memphis. With Brenda's medical condition, the convenience of attending church in our new neighborhood was appealing. We felt the church was a place where our family could reach out and promote racial harmony. We decided to visit a church located in close proximity to our home one Sunday morning. We were warmly greeted by several members as well as the pastor and were invited back, so we returned numerous times. The pastor was a large, balding, generous man who conveyed a fatherly and compassionate persona. He shook my hand without hesitation. He visited our home on several occasions and prayed with us. Brenda and I attended the early Sunday morning service and became involved in an early morning Sunday school class we enjoyed. After church and Sunday school, we would have dinner at places like Piccadilly's or Ryan's, where we all loved the cafeteria-style menu. Brenda and I decided to join this church. Eighteen months later, the pastor abruptly announced his retirement without explanation. Rumors circulated that he was forced out because of his inclusive philosophy, welcoming all to the church who wanted to hear the gospel of Jesus Christ and accept him as their personal savior. It was this man and his philosophy that appealed to my family; once he departed, the coldness my family and I experienced in our neighborhood became more and more obvious among other church members. Apparently, several families followed the pastor and his ministry to another nearby town to start another church. Those left behind were apparently the architects of the pastor's early retirement. It was not long before my family and I felt unwelcome, so we moved on.

We visited other churches, mostly African American, but never felt truly welcome. Exclusivity on a different level was practiced at these churches, with the litmus test being if you were a native, bred and raised in Memphis. Conversation usually did not progress once it was clear that you were not a native Memphian. If you were, a more inclusive world was opened to you. A shocking, unexpected experience for me was that the same coldness I felt directed toward me in white churches was also present in the majority of the black churches we revisited. The few who would approach us and engage in conversation—almost always older women—encouraged us to stay strong as a family. They seemed to get it. The look in the eyes of these women, often tearing up, one hand on mine, the other on Brenda's, said that they truly understood the stress of caring for a disabled spouse. These women were exceptional cooks and often presented us with their very best treats: homemade pound cake, sweet potato pie, pecan pie! Even today, I can close my eyes and imagine the rich aromas, which often triggered memories of the flavors and smells of Big Mama's cooking. These moments were the rare beams of hope generated in an increasingly darkening existence. My wife, children, and I found refuge at home, our castle into which we all escaped to rest our weary souls from the constant negative messages outside.

Thankfully, I had earned the professional respect of my peers, as well as of the doctors in training. By 1992, I had published solely or in collaboration with other fellow radiologists at least twelve scientific papers, and one chapter in the clinics of medicine periodical. I was on my way to being promoted to associate professor, hopefully with tenure. My compensation was adequate for a university professor, and I also remained convinced that I would not receive an opportunity to practice within one of the private practice radiology groups. This feeling was reinforced by some of my peers in the UT radiology department, namely the white males who thought Memphis would never support African American radiologists in what was considered the mainstream of private radiology practice. Black radiologists from other cities I met at CME meetings concurred. The African American doctors in Memphis thought and recommended that I try to join one of the all-white radiology groups in Memphis; otherwise, I should be content to remain at the university radiology practice. Some of them further stated that they were reluctant to support the practice of another doctor who would probably make more money than they did. This response, coming from fellow African American doctors, was particularly painful to hear. Yet, all of these physicians supported white radiology practices.

Even though most of the time life seemed stagnant in Memphis, there were signs developing signaling the coming of the winds of change that would affect all levels of life including business, politics, medicine, and professional sports. Memphis had just elected its first black mayor; an African American held the ninth district Congressional seat. A little-known governor of Arkansas was elected to the presidency of the United States in the fall of 1992. Significant economic growth occurred nationally. Memphis was becoming a national distribution center for many businesses thanks to Federal Express. And yes, change came to Memphis radiology. I was approached and offered a position with a large, prestigious radiology group. Brenda and I discussed this opportunity, and I accepted the offer. I did not realize the magnitude of my decision initially, but I had become the first African American radiologist to join a major private practice in Memphis. This improbable occurrence shocked many naysayers in the Memphis medical community. As gratifying as this event was for me, even more gratifying was the discussion I had with one of my partners several years later. He said, "Jim, you were voted into our group unanimously. We hired you because you were and are one of the best radiologists in Memphis, not just the best African American radiologist." I felt that I had always tried to approach life in a color-blind fashion, whereas it seemed that all attitudes and decisions made by anyone on a daily basis were flavored heavily by race. My partner's comment was more than refreshing. For me, it confirmed that the winds of change had deeply affected this radiology group. These men and women were committed to integrity with high moral and social standards. I felt honored to be among them. The dream that Dr. King had brought to Memphis in 1968 had traveled through the years, riding on the winds of change. Soon after I joined this group, I attended a special dinner honoring one of the retiring partners. He pulled me aside and said to me, "Jim, congratulations. I know that Memphis has not been very kind to you or your family. You deserve this opportunity; you have earned it."

Private practice was extremely busy for me. I worked hard; I was dedicated and loyal. I accepted any and all requests for my professional time and body-imaging expertise. My personal life had become even more demanding and highly stressful. Brenda's MS was progressing with increased frequency of relapses. Each relapse left her weaker and weaker. Steroid therapy no longer worked as well. By 1998, Brenda began to fall with increasing frequency. Many mornings I received frantic calls from Brenda for help, which necessitated turning around in traffic and going back home while on my way to the hospital, or leaving the hospital to go home to assist her. Previously, she had been adamant about not hiring an assistant because she did not want strangers in our home. As a result, I was becoming increasingly angry, frustrated, and stressed.

Once she finally agreed to hire daytime help, I was somewhat relieved and less stressed. Then, the calls for my assistance started again. The agency helpers could not physically lift her after a fall. It was an impossible situation—how could I practice medicine? One evening after I arrived home from the hospital, Brenda fell, striking her head and face against one of the night stands in our bedroom. I rushed her to the emergency room. The CT examination demonstrated non-displaced fractures involving her left maxillary sinus. Fortunately, there were no other injuries. I decided that it was time for Brenda to use her wheelchair full-time for safety reasons. We would also need full-time caregivers to be with her while I was at the hospital. There were no family or friends in the Memphis area available to assist us, and Courtney and Van were full-time college students.

Brenda's personality began to deteriorate. She became more and more demanding and disagreeable. Many of the home health care workers sent to our home resigned or quit citing her nasty attitude as the reason usually. Brenda could be difficult, controlling, and inflexible. We had many arguments and confrontations regarding these issues during our marriage. Her explanation was always the same: "I can't help it, I'm just like my mother." So, yes, I was manipulated by her behavior, usually allowing her to have her way more and more as her disease progressed. One of the most contentious, stressful issues was getting her to wear incontinence diapers. From 1998 until September 2001, it was not uncommon for me to be awakened several times during the night to assist her to the bathroom. On a good night, I managed to get three to four hours of sleep. The nights I was on call were especially horrendous as I was usually up all night dealing with emergency issues as well as personal care for Brenda. My days were full, my nights even fuller. I was also the scheduler for our practice, responsible for staffing the hospitals and outpatient practices we serviced with an adequate number of radiology physicians (my partners). It was also my responsibility to schedule vacations. I was a member of our group's Board of Directors, served on several hospital committees, and was actively involved in our resident/physician training program. I cooked most of the evening meals at home. I took care of all of our financial matters. Yet, I never thought that I was overextended. I felt that I possessed an endless supply of physical and mental stamina. To many people, I was that little engine that did not and would not quit. My nickname at work was the "Mule": one possessing the temperament and desire to carry heavy burdens. I had never learned how to say no

By 2000, I started to notice a difference in how I perceived my surroundings. My little-boy view of the world had long since been clouded by my life experiences. Certainly, the years had tempered my outlook and expectations and, I thought, helped develop some degree of maturity regarding my attitude and outlook. However, I still had childlike notions that everyone could read my mind and see the big flashing neon sign I carried around saying, "I am overworked at home and in my medical practice. I am a good citizen, I pay taxes; please help me!" When asked, "How are you doing, Jim? How are things at home?" my reply was always, "I am well and my family is doing fine." By September of 2001, I had reached my breaking point. I could no longer hide my true feelings and emotions. One day at work, I cried when asked how I was doing by one of my partners. I wanted to get off of the endless treadmill I felt I was on. My outlook had darkened; the boundless energy that propelled me through prior life challenges was gone.

My partners, who were aware of my situation, suggested that I take time off to rest and implement measures for my situation. I desperately needed help at home. For many years Brenda had been unable to cook, clean, perform errands, or help with financial matters, including paying bills. I did all of this and could not do it any longer. The next day, September 11, 2001, I was still in bed near mid-day when my son burst into my bedroom shouting, "Dad, turn on the television. Something horrible is happening! Terrorists are attacking the United States! They just flew a plane into the World Trade Center!"

I flipped the TV on. All channels were broadcasting a special report. Debate raged as to whether this was a terrorist attack or just a horrible accident. Suddenly, a second airliner crashed into the second tower of the World Trade Center! Quickly, additional reports of airliners crashing into the Pentagon and in Pennsylvania were reported. *Damn*! I thought as I was mesmerized by events unfolding before my eyes. *What if these planes had been carrying nuclear weapons*? My current situation, while serious enough, paled in comparison to these national events: thousands of people had just lost their lives, leaving behind their loved ones who would be emotionally scarred for life. I got up and prayed, thanking God that I was alive and that my family was safe.

Still, all was not well. I was encouraged to seek professional psychiatric help. I got a referral to a psychiatrist with a good reputation. I sat in the waiting area at this psychiatrist's office dreading the repercussions I was sure would follow: people would talk, despite confidentiality rules: "Hey, did you hear about Jim? He had to see a shrink! Well, I guess he was too weak to handle his own problems. How is he going to continue practicing? He is unstable." What would I do then?

My negative thoughts were suddenly interrupted by the nurse. "Dr. Ellis, Dr. Banner will see you now." Dr. Banner appeared, shook my hand, and welcomed me into his office. He was as advertised: friendly, insightful, helpful, professional, and extremely intelligent. We talked about my situation currently, my past and my outlook. Dr. Banner asked, "Jim, you are suffering from depression." This statement stunned me. "What are your thoughts?" he added.

After a brief period of silence, I replied, "I can't be! Doctors don't get depressed, do they?"

Dr. Banner smiled. "Yes, Jim, we are just like everyone else. We are not immune to disease or illness, whether it be cancer, stroke, or heart attack, and yes, we as doctors get depressed too. In fact, doctors are vulnerable because of the constant high level of stress they experience throughout their careers. That is why it is so important to have outlets for stress like exercise, sports, and relaxation. A well-balanced diet as well as rest and time off are also essential. Do you have a hobby, Jim?"

I shrugged, "Not really. I like exercise, playing basketball, reading, and playing games like chess. I just don't have the time to enjoy any of it. My plate is full at work and at home."

"Jim, one of the first changes I want you to make is to make time for yourself," replied Dr. Banner. "Otherwise, you are going to burn out, get sick, or die. If that happens, there won't be anyone to do the things you are doing now, including caring for your wife."

"Dr. Banner, my wife is spoiled, narcissistic, and very possessive; she seems to be getting worse as her disease progresses. I pay for in-home care but most people quit because of her nasty attitude. One agency caregiver got so angry with her that she poured salt on the sheets of our bed on her side! I was told that this is akin to cursing someone, if you believe that sort of thing. More often than not, agency caregivers wished us harm or ill will."

"I know that must be frustrating for you, but you need to promise me that you will find a way to get respite care help or time off for yourself. I would also strongly urge you to decrease or cease extra duties such as administrative duties at work."

I replied, "Okay. I will."

He pressed further. "Additionally, I am prescribing an antidepressant that should help you. So we'll see you next week, okay?"

"Next week. Okay." I returned home and began making the necessary phone calls to end my administrative obligations at work. I resigned from the Board of Directors and all hospital committees and relinquished the scheduler position for my group. I reduced my night-call obligations by taking a salary cut. I was firm with Brenda about the use of incontinence diapers at bedtime so that I could get some much-needed rest during the night. The first night following these changes, I experienced the most restful sleep that I had experienced for at least three years! By the end of the seven days off I was given to address my issues, I had improved. I was rested, more hopeful, and energetic. I hired a personal chef to prepare the evening meals. I made time for exercise and started playing golf. I was able to contact several home health care agencies, interview potential caregivers, and hire someone who Brenda was comfortable with. Finally, I returned to work.

My therapy sessions continued to be successful. I learned about depression and its treatment. However, I did not want to be labeled as a depressed person. I was a doctor, and doctors more readily accepted physical illnesses than mental ones—*hell, what will the referring doctors think?* I wondered. Would they think I was a failure? I was not tough enough to withstand the stress. I would not be considered a part of the club, the medical fraternity, whose message was not supportive of doctors affected by a psychiatric illnesses. I discussed these negative thoughts with Dr. Banner, who reassured me it would not be that way. We discussed many aspects of my life, including my marriage. I explained to him how difficult Brenda could be, how possessive and controlling she was. One example I gave him was how she always attempted to sabotage my continuing medical education trips by pretending to be sick, declaring an emergency to get me home early. Usually this manipulative behavior started on the second day of a five-day medical meeting. These courses are mandatory for doctors to maintain a medical license in good standing with the medical board; one must provide documentation of twenty to thirty hours of CME per year. Hospital privileges required documented CME hours as well. Dr. Banner seemed to understand my frustration. I also explained to him how frustrating it is to travel with anyone needing a wheelchair full time. In the past, I attempted several

CME trips with Brenda; all were nightmares. We traveled with her own private wheelchair, which was often misplaced by the airline or taken by others disembarking from the plane. On one of these trips the covered mobile walkway malfunctioned, requiring passengers to disembark from the airplane on an old uncovered mobile staircase. Fortunately, Brenda was light enough for me to carry her off the plane and down the staircase. In spite of these limitations, I tried hard.

Dr. Banner sensed the guilt in my voice. My eyes welled with tears as he said, "Jim, you need to take control of your life. You deserve to be treated with respect. You need to create your own space; you need time for yourself. What have you decided about a hobby?"

I replied, "I have decided to try golf."

"Sounds good; good luck! You know it can be a frustrating game

"Several of my partners play golf, so perhaps I can socialize more with them through this game," I said.

He nodded. "Give me an update during our next session. In the meantime, continue your routine of exercise, healthy diet, and controlling stress. You need to insist on taking time for yourself. Remember, there is only one you. Without you, your family won't have that rock, that anchor that they all need. They need you healthy, Jim."

I started playing golf during a part of my day off. Most of my partners were members of prestigious country clubs with golf courses, but I played at the public courses in the Memphis area. I could not afford to make the large financial commitment that the country clubs required. I read a short golf instructional book and purchased some used equipment, with the rest supplied by my brother, an avid golfer. I frequented a golf driving range to practice when I could not get a tee time at my favorite golf course, Galloway. I must confess my initial feeling about golf was that it was an easy game, made for old and fat people. How wrong I was! Professional and skilled amateur golfers play so effortlessly, giving the observer the false sense that the game is easy. My early golf outings were atrocious, but I had fun. It had been many years since I had been outside for an extended period of time for my own enjoyment. I was at peace, serene in a serene setting. I really did not care much about my score—I was a true bogey golfer. My scores started in the low hundreds and gradually improved to mid eighties. My best score was a seventy-nine at Galloway. I walked the course whenever I could, which was great exercise! I also purchased Nautilus equipment for in-home workouts. I joined an exercise facility, working out on my day off when I was not playing golf. My follow-up therapy sessions went well; Dr. Banner noticed that my mood and outlook were vastly improved, my life seemed to be going well.

Gradually, I became more and more convinced that I did not have a mental illness, but rather had experienced situational depression. I was cured. I had weathered this storm of my life. Dr. Banner and I discussed whether I would need drug therapy indefinitely. I was stable, having made the necessary lifestyle changes, and was thriving. I decided that I no longer needed therapy; I had done everything Dr. Banner asked me to do except for one thing: addressing my marital issues, including the constant struggle with Brenda for some control over my personal space. She wanted to control every aspect of my life, to know my whereabouts every minute of every day. I felt that it was time for me to seize control of my life. I took a stand and said no to the continual verbal and mental abuse; I wanted my freedom. I decided to move out and file for divorce by the fall of 2003. I felt that this was the only way I could finally gain control of my life.

Chapter 7

Trail to Decline

My decision surprised my son and daughter, but not the few people in whom I had confided about my marital difficulties. They had heard the stories of how cold and hateful Brenda could be to me, how demanding she was, how she belittled me and ridiculed me constantly. Courtney and Van were adults with their own lives. I moved to an apartment three miles from my home in Germantown. I paid for round-the-clock in-home care for Brenda. Within a few months, I was served at work with divorce papers from Brenda. I had hoped that an amicable settlement could be reached. I was willing to give up everything, only requesting enough money to survive. I soon discovered the real intent of her divorce action: not to divorce at all, but rather legally separate. The terms were such that I would not have any freedom of all. I would be required to get her up and ready in the morning at 6 a.m., drive her to various medical, dental, and beauty salon appointments, guarantee her meals, run errands, and take care of all financial matters. The only difference from my pre-divorced life was where I slept.

I followed a grueling schedule for one year, beginning at 5 a.m. At 6 a.m. I went to check on Brenda every day and assist with bathing her, dressing her, and preparing breakfast. I was done at the hospital by 6 p.m. most days unless I was on call for the night. My life was reverting back to the routine preceding my first depression. It was during this period that I turned to alcohol for relief, for that sense of ease and comfort. I decided to explore the benefits of wine and rather quickly decided that this was the epicurean elixir I needed. I enjoyed white wine, particularly chardonnay. My routine was to enjoy a glass with dinner, then one glass before retiring. Wine helped me relax and seemed to elevate my mood. I also slept soundly, better than I had in years. I started collecting high-quality chardonnays such as Ramey and Cakebread. I also started to attend wine-tasting events. I met many interesting people at these events, including several women with whom I developed close relationships. I needed to be touched, held, and loved.

The vast majority of my free time was spent taking care of issues for Brenda and working for extra pay within my medical practice. Twenty-four-hour care for Brenda was expensive, and not covered by insurance. Lawyer fees from attorneys working on our divorce were in excess of $5000 per month. By the beginning of 2005, my stress level reached new heights. Brenda discovered that I was seeing other women and became furious. There seem to be this constant battle for my time from Brenda and the other women. I soon realized that I could not please them all. I was getting extreme pressure from my son and daughter and Brenda's relatives to end the divorce proceedings and return home. My wife and her attorney agreed to drop their divorce action if I return home and made an honest attempt to salvage my marriage. I must admit that I had become cynical about the institution of marriage. The discovery of my wife's infidelity early in our marriage, her constant hateful demeanor, the extreme stress of physician training and medical practice, and the high divorce rate among my peers were the basis for much of this cynicism. However, I decided to return home and make another attempt at saving my marriage. I returned home to resume my marriage as a fully devoted husband. I was determined to do all that I could do for peace and harmony to return to our family.

Our family was blessed with a wonderful event in 2005: the engagement and marriage of our daughter Courtney. Michael and Courtney met while she was a student at Vanderbilt Law School in Nashville. It was love at first sight. The two dated seriously throughout law school and got engaged in early 2005, with a planned early December wedding. We all were immediately fond of Michael. He carried himself well. His strong, quiet personality was a good fit for my daughter. He was also a golfer, and introduced my daughter to golf. His personal dream was to become a professional golfer. The planned wedding day, December 5, seemed to arrive in no time. My daughter was a picture-perfect bride, lovely in every way. I hated the thought of losing my little girl, but could not think of a better man than the one she chose as her husband. The ceremony and reception were held at the Racquet Club. Family, friends, many of my physician partners, many of Courtney's fellow attorneys as well as other associates from her law firm, and others attended with joy. I am sure that this was one of the most harmonious gatherings of doctors and lawyers I (and many others) have ever witnessed. Everyone including Brenda, Van, and I experienced what I felt was the event of our lives. The newlyweds traveled to Hawaii for their honeymoon. Brenda and I recalled our humble beginning, and thanked God that we were able to give our daughter such a grand start to married life.

When 2005 ended, I had completed one year trying desperately to rebuild my marriage. Brenda remained distant; basically, we tolerated each other. The nights, however, were a cruel reminder of how vicious and nasty Brenda's personality was still. Nearly every night, I was awakened by temper tantrums about other women I had been involved with. She reminded me of all the mistakes I had made. And so it went, on and on for hours each night. I began to feel myself sliding back into the dark world I had escaped from in 2001.

Slowly but progressively, the progress I had made since my depression was diagnosed in 2001 had been severely eroded, and I was letting it happen. I felt alone, watching life march on without me. I had reverted back to my old habits, putting myself last, abandoning the daily structure that had worked so well. More and more, I felt pressed for time. I started cutting corners, shortening my exercise routine. I began to cook more meals to save money rather than continuing the personal chef service. I began to work extra on weekends to earn additional income to help pay for home healthcare for Brenda. I reasoned that other families with similar care issues managed the stress, so I needed to find a way to do it. I told myself, *You're a smart person, a doctor associated with a successful medical practice. You have been trained to solve problems. There must be a way to do it without losing your sanity. You're not depressed, just stressed.* I needed to dig deeper and find those resources within me that helped me reach the professional success I had achieved. In spite of these positive thoughts, though, darker thoughts persisted. It seemed that the core part of me kept telling me that I was losing this battle. The rest of me could not and would not accept losing anything. I believed that where there is a will, there is a way; I practiced this and seemed to win with this can-do attitude.

I tried desperately to will my way through the largest crisis in my life. I convinced myself that I did not need help from anyone, that I would overcome this battle by myself. My denial was strong that I was not depressed nor did I need medication. All I needed was chardonnay.

January 2007 greeted me with more bad news. I received a phone call in the middle of a stressful day from Brenda. She reported to me that she had fallen awkwardly to the floor while being transferred from her wheelchair to her sitting chair. She stated that she was fine. I completed my day at the hospital and arrived home. Brenda was sitting in her recliner. She pointed to her lower right leg, which was slightly swollen. A large bruise was also present. My instincts told me that this was more than a simple fall and skin bruise. I suspected that she had fractured her leg. I touched her leg and asked her, "Does that hurt?"

She shrugged. "Not really. I guess it's just a bad bruise. However, the agency caregiver and I heard a loud pop sound when I fell."

I had heard enough. I replied, "Honey, I think you broke your leg. I need to get you to the hospital right away!" I loaded Brenda into our car and went to the Germantown Presbyterian Hospital emergency room. X-rays confirmed a spiral fracture of her right tibia. They put a cast on the leg and referred us to an orthopedic surgeon for management. He advised us that the healing process for the fracture may be somewhat prolonged because of Brenda's immobility. Bone stimulation treatments could help promote the healing process.

Caring for a totally disabled person is challenging; imagine increasing the challenge or level of difficulty by the addition of a plaster leg cast from above the knee to the toes. I was so fearful that Brenda would be dropped again during a transfer that I contemplated a prolonged leave of absence so that I could be home to assist her. I spent several sleepless nights knowing that somehow I needed to be home during this current period, but I could not afford unpaid leave from work. Then, an alternative idea occurred to me. Technologically, advances in radiology had made the specialty filmless; that is, X-ray images were presented on a large monitor rather than on hard copy film. This new image presentation is a component of PACS (personal archival computer system). PACS allows instantaneous viewing and interpretation of radiology studies off-site, which made working from home as a radiologist a reality. I discussed this option with my partners. I was surprised that they accepted this idea and wanted it to be implemented immediately. I would read and interpret radiology studies from 2 p.m. to 9 p.m., which made the evening workload less onerous for partners working the 5 p.m. to 11 p.m. shift at the hospital. Working from home did ease my stress level concerning Brenda's safety. However, because I was readily available, I was frequently asked to cook, clean, shop, and perform additional errands including transporting Brenda to a multitude of doctor visits (orthopedic, internal medicine, gynecology, neurology, ophthalmology, and radiology/mammography). In the past, I had used my day off to accomplish many of these tasks as well as self-care issues like exercise and relaxation. I was completely surprised by a phone call from one of my partners informing me that my day off had been rescinded because of jealousy by certain group members regarding my work-from-home status. It was explained to me that taking away my day off was viewed as a fair trade-off for the luxury of working from home. I was flabbergasted, hurt, and angry all at once. I thought it was selfish and mean-spirited for my partners to feel this way. I was a very productive member of our group, and maintained my productivity while working from home, verified by several assessments of my work productivity. I wondered what other penalties would be forthcoming—no vacation, perhaps? Additionally, they cut back on a crucial medical benefit, which in the past helped ease some of the financial burden of home healthcare for Brenda. The net result was a tax increase and less take-home income. It seemed many of my partners were very vocal about fairness and were extremely resentful of anything that appeared to give any partner a perceived advantage.

By 2007, our group had grown to more than forty-five members. Most received much higher starting salaries than I had and were made full partners much sooner than I. They functioned by the doctrine, "Give me more and I will give you less." One memorable comment I had heard from one of our newly hired partners was, "I am not paid as much as a full partner so no one should expect me to generate more income than I am paid." I had worked extremely hard as a young member of our group, generating much more income than I was paid, and I continued this work ethic up to my last day working. I can say that I was not surprised to learn that many of the younger members were not supportive of me working from home and insisted on me losing my day off. Even some of my senior partners didn't support me, although I thought that they would be more familiar with my wife's disability and the challenges of in-home nursing care for her, complicated by the presence of a fractured leg. In spite of this attitude, referring physicians enthusiastically praised the swing shift I covered, especially those from the emergency room. Near real-time radiology interpretation was providing significant improvements in patient care.

By June 2007 my needs, particularly my demand for the return of my day off and a medical benefit that would allow the use of pre-tax dollars for Brenda's care, continued to be ignored. Each day and night appeared to progress faster and faster approaching the point of a blurred existence, a continuous treadmill of work, caregiving, and stress, without a break, without rest or respite. I continued to feel that uneasiness of slipping back into darkness mounting.

The second week of August, I received a phone call from Dr. Fritz, a young radiologist trained by our residency program. He was one of the best and I was proud to have helped train him. We hired him into our group practice after the completion of his residency training. After a short time, he decided to leave our practice for another radiology practice whose location better fit his active lifestyle. He updated me on this new practice and told me he and his wife were expecting their first child, which delighted me. Dr. Fritz was my hero. His quick action had saved the life of a patient involved in a CT scan accident. The accident was unfortunate because it was preventable: a CT tech failed to check the dye injector prior to its use. The injector was filled with approximately 100 mL of air rather than dye so that during the scan, the injector delivered this air into the patient—potentially a lethal event. Dr. Fritz's quick thinking and action saved the patient's life. The patient recovered after a short stay in the intensive care unit. Some weeks after this incident, I was called to attend an impromptu meeting regarding the recent dismissal of the most experienced and respected senior CT technician in the department of radiology; several of my partners called the meeting to appeal to keep his job. I did not know why he had been terminated until the meeting commenced. We all spoke highly of this gentleman and his expertise, and pleaded for his reinstatement. Two hospital administrators protested adamantly that he not be reinstated, and proceeded to disclose why. We were told that the CT tech responsible for the air injection mistake recorded all of her conversations after the incident, including an extremely derogatory racial comment made by this senior tech. He apparently said, "You know that CT accident you were involved in is a good way to kill some niggers!" (The patient was African American.) The meeting room became eerily silent, enough almost to hear the pounding heartbeats of everyone present.

The silence was broken by one of the hospital administrators, who happened to be African American. "The comments this gentleman made were insulting, demeaning, and callous. He is not welcome to work for us no matter how talented or qualified he is. He will not be retained. Thanks for your input."

The meeting ended and I walked out feeling a myriad of emotions: confusion, anger, hurt, surprise, disgust, and betrayal. My opinion of this tech was that he was the consummate professional; I knew of no complaints regarding his interactions with peers or patients. Several days passed. I received a phone call at home from this gentleman. I listened as he repeatedly apologized for the disparaging comments he had made. He began crying. Through the sobs he asked for my forgiveness. He expressed how this situation had changed his view of the world and opinions of other people. He apologized for allowing and encouraging his children to view African Americans so negatively, saying that in his household, the word nigger was always used to describe any African American, including athletes, Congressmen, absolutely anyone: to his family, they were all just niggers. He again pleaded for my forgiveness. He stated that his family and he were forever changed. He said, "That word is now banned in my house forever."

I responded, "I forgive you. I hope that your new outlook will be a positive influence to your family, friends, and others. I wish you well. I appreciate your honesty and your new commitment to fairness and teaching others not to hate."

He replied, "Thank you, and God bless you, Dr. Ellis."

Dr. Fritz and I continued talking about his new practice. He felt that everything was perfect. When not working, he and his wife enjoyed the many outdoor activities available to them. He inquired about the radiology practice and how I was doing. I described the recent addition of PACS as well as new multislice CT equipment, and then talked about working from home and the reason why.

Dr. Fritz began, "Dr. Ellis …"

I interrupted, "Please call me Jim."

"Okay, I will, but it is my way of showing you respect."

"Thank you. May I address you by your first name—David, right?"

"Please," he said. Then he continued, "Jim, I know how stressful your life is with the responsibilities of a disabled wife and a busy medical practice. I don't think I could last one day in your shoes. With all that you have to deal with, my wife and I often wonder how you deal with all the racial stuff there."

I replied, "There is racism everywhere."

"Yes, but it is so blatant there," he said. "That incident involving the senior CT tech and the racist comments he made is just the tip of the iceberg. People there behave totally differently when you're not around. The black radiology techs are treated horribly. They are given the worst job assignments and are often denied deserving advancement or promotions. Worst of all, the N-word is used by their white peers and superiors. Everything, every minute of every day, is about race and how to avoid African Americans. My wife and I got sick of it. Whoever takes a stand and refuses to accept this behavior as the norm is ostracized. It's like a big country club; if you don't follow the rules, you can't be a member of the club. My wife and I didn't want to raise our children in such a narrow-minded, hateful environment."

"Wow!" I remarked. "Do you really think so?"

Dr. Fritz sighed, "Jim, believe me, you never see it because everyone is on their best behavior when they are around you. As long as you produce two to three times what you are paid, you will always get the proverbial slap on the back of approval. That is pretty insulting to take away partner benefits such as your day off and the medical benefit for your wife without offering an alternative or replacement for this benefit. Have you thought about relocating? Would you consider moving to join my practice?"

I responded, "Thank you. It's tempting. I have so much of my life invested here. I would hate to give up and leave. I guess I am a stubborn old man."

"I understand, but let's keep in touch," he agreed.

"Okay. Listen, thank you for calling. It is always a pleasure to hear from you. Thank you for the enlightening discussion about my situation here. I will seriously consider your offer, so thank you for thinking of me. And congratulations to you and your wife for her pregnancy. I know that both of you are excited and I am also for you." We hung up.

What an interesting conversation, I thought to myself. I spoke with several of the African American radiology technicians about their racial experience in the department. Some were afraid to make any comments; the few who did related that their racial experience was and remained bad. They told me of discriminatory practices based upon race, such as undesirable job assignments and use of racial slurs. As incredible as their stories were to me, even more incredible stories from a couple of fair-minded white radiology techs confirmed the stories. Soon,

I was approached by individuals who indicated that they were tired of the status quo regarding race relations in the radiology department, and commended me for being interested. Without asking, I was given the phone number of the woman who had taped the conversation and racial remarks made by the senior technologist who was fired. I called her, and was surprised when she told me that she was forced to leave Memphis because of death threats she had received! She did not divulge her new location to me because of her fear for her safety. She did tell me that she was still in possession of the tape recording but feared coming forward with it. I thanked her for talking with me and wished her well.

I hung up the phone and felt a coldness envelop me. My mood and spirit sank. The light in the dark room was flickering and dimming, and becoming dimmer and dimmer; it had developed a reddish hue, likely related to my intensifying anger. I thought about the patient, an African American, nearly killed by medical equipment and human error in the radiology department. I thought about the outrageous racial comment made, about how comfortable the individual felt making such comments in public. This comment spoke volumes about the mindset of many individuals in the radiology department who were responsible for the safety and welfare of black patients in their care. I remembered a recent incident involving another African American patient whose colon was perforated by the vigorous insertion of a barium enema tube. Was that another example of the callous attitude and hatred? How many individuals in the radiology department harbored the same feelings of raw hatred? Did any of my partners think this way? The senior tech responsible for the disparaging racial remarks was a close friend and golfing buddy of several members of the radiology department; I wondered if they all shared the same racist views and thoughts.

I could not help but think back to those times early in my career when racial hatred seemed to be the accepted norm in society, including medical workers and physicians. My hiring by an all-white private radiology practice, a first in Memphis in 1993, signaled to me the start of an era of enlightenment, when race would not matter. Perhaps I had been blinded by the smiles and, yes, the respect I received from everyone. Black radiology technicians never approached me concerning any racial mistreatment. As I saw things, the racial pulse of the radiology department favored equal opportunity and treatment for all. I became angry, mostly at myself for not seeing the real state of racial relations in the radiology department. I felt like a complete failure. What I thought I represented—a positive image, a role model—meant nothing. Attitudes were still as narrow-minded as they were over thirty years ago when I first encountered them in medical school. Everyone, both black and white, still went home every day and perpetuated negative thoughts and imagery to their children about the other race. I had the epiphany that no matter how expert I was, in the eyes of my white counterparts and families, I was still just another nigger.

A flood of memories of past negative experiences overwhelmed me. I was a failure, besieged in my own home. I failed because I was not strong enough to fight off the heavy load of depression and emotions! I felt helpless, alone, and ostracized. I was alone in the dark room I had entered. I had a glass of wine, then another, without relief. My flickering flame of hope was dimming rapidly. I had no answers for my situation. I thought about the suicides I knew about personally, in college, medical school, and residency. Was suicide the answer? I had been taught never to express any emotions, but heavy streams of tears rolled from my eyes, cascading over my cheeks and lips, dripping like a steady rain onto my shirt and lap. I started my life journey not ever feeling limited by race, poverty, welfare, a fatherless home—not limited by anything or anyone. That drive, that sense of mission, was rapidly dying right here, right now. Multiple life crises, an increasingly hostile work environment, and intense financial strain presented a wall of issues facing me that I could not see beyond. I had no answers, no solutions. I had no support pillars. Was suicide the answer? It became extremely clear to me that yes, suicide was the answer. I could no longer tolerate the torment from everywhere and from everyone. Soon, there was pitch black darkness. I did not know what dimension I had entered.

911: "What is the nature of your call?"

Caller: "I just killed my wife, and now I'm going to kill myself!"

911: "Sir? Sir! Listen; please don't hang up!"

Caller: "Goodbye."

Chapter 8

Alive or Dead

"Sir. Sir, can you hear me?"

"Where ... am I?"

"You are at the trauma center, the Med. You have been shot. Do you understand?"

"Where am I? What happened?"

The nurse's voice sounded far away. "You were shot by the police twice, once in your mouth, once in your left arm."

I couldn't process the information at first. "What? ... Oh, God! I wanted to die! I tried to commit suicide! I guess I failed, or am I on the other side? ... I am! I am on the other side!"

The nurse said, "No sir, you are still alive, still here."

I groaned. "I want to die! I want to die! Please let me die! Please!" Then, I felt pain, increasing pain in my left arm. I touched my face using my right hand. My finger touched a gaping hole directly below my nose, midline. "Oh, my God!"

The nurse replied, "You are a very lucky man. The shot to your face should have killed you. It appears that your front teeth stopped or deflected the bullet. The shot to your arm missed the artery and humerus. I guess it was not your time to go, sir."

My next memory was of part of my stay in the Memphis Mental Health Institute, a state-run psychiatric hospital. I was heavily medicated for most of my forty-five-day stay. It took me several days to accept that I was in serious trouble. Once my mental evaluation was completed, I was to be incarcerated and formally charged. My daughter Courtney, an attorney, selected a defense team for me. We all met, and they informed me of the serious charges I faced: two counts of attempted first-degree murder. I was stunned. I could not remember any details of my encounter with the police. My lawyers informed me that I fired a weapon at the police and they returned fire, hitting me twice. I was sick and needed mental help that was long overdue.

Courtney arranged to have me transferred to a highly regarded institute that specialized in treating psychiatric illnesses. "Dad, the name of the recovery institute is Ridgeview, in Atlanta. It's considered one of the best. This is what is best for you, Daddy. We all love you and want you to recover. Mom, Van, and all of us love you, Dad," she said, holding my hand as she teared up. "I want my daddy back!" Courtney and the other attorneys reassured me that they would take care of my personal affairs and arrange for in-home care for Brenda. One of Courtney's partners said, "Jim, we want you to concentrate on yourself, concentrate on your recovery."

I started to cry. "Thank you. I want to pick up the pieces of my life and become whole again." As I spoke these words, I wondered if I would ever recover from such a devastating life crisis. I thought, *Is this a dream? Yes, maybe this is all a dream. I've had dreams before that were so realistic, as real as my life now—so yes, that's it, this is all a dream! I will wake up any minute now, be thankful that I was just having a nightmare.*

I reached up to touch my lip and once again felt the deformity (the gaping hole had been repaired at the trauma center). I felt the broken, jagged edges of several broken front teeth and the gaps from missing or partially missing teeth. Courtney whispered "Don't worry, Dad, it all can be fixed." We both had tears rolling down our faces as we held hands. "You were and are still a wonderful dad to me. It is time for me to help you! I want you alive, to see your grandchildren!" We stood and hugged. I shook hands with the other attorneys, and then the meeting ended.

That night, I began to experience horrible nightmares of death and destruction. I saw no recognizable faces, just scores of featureless humanoid forms tormented by a huge creature. I awoke from this dream screaming and sweating. The nightmares continued, interrupting my sleep many nights. The result was insomnia, as usually I could not fall back to sleep after one of the dreams. So I would lay awake, afraid to go back to sleep, but also afraid of what the next day would bring, feeling hopeless about my situation. I had a mental illness; I was depressed and suicidal. This place, this moment in time was all real. Scenes from my life, especially the successful times, played through my head. James Ellis, the little boy who was conceived and born in Chattanooga, with boundless energy and that can-do spirit, ending up in a psychiatric facility, charged with a serious crime. I re-entered that dark room and returned to the world of suicidal ideation. I promised myself that the next time I would succeed. I was placed on suicide watch for the duration of my stay at the Memphis Mental Health Institute.

Occasionally, I reached to touch my mouth wound as well as my arm wound. Both were healing but were depressing reminders of my failed suicide attempt and the police shooting I had survived. Why had I survived two fatal shots? I would have been better off if I had died rather than experience the living hell I currently resided in. *How bizarre*, I thought; *I meant to commit suicide, but now I'm charged with committing a crime.* I could not remember calling 911 or shooting at the police. My psychiatrist at Memphis Mental Health felt I was temporarily incompetent or insane at the time of these events, but in spite of antidepressant therapy and psychiatric counseling, I continued to fantasize about suicide.

I received visits from family including my children and my sister Janice. Several physicians from my radiology group also visited. I was always energized by these visits, but once they left, I returned to the dark room and suicidal thoughts. I did manage to read a book one of my partners gave me: *John Adams*, the biography of the second president, by author David McCullough. Somehow, I found the mental energy to read this six hundred-page novel. I became captivated by Adams' life experiences and how he coped with the many issues of his time, including his own depression. I admired his courage and belief in fairness as well as the equality of all men. I learned that he and his wife did not own slaves. In fact, they educated and freed every slave given to them. He found enslavement and relentless hatred of blacks to be morally wrong, a sin in his eyes. He was truly a man of the highest moral character and integrity, and certainly, he was a highly educated and accomplished man, but he too appeared to suffer from depression most of his adult life. He lived with it, fought it, living to the age of ninety. *What was his secret? How did he do it? What sustained him during those quiet, dark predawn hours?* I asked myself. I wondered if he ever faltered and considered suicide. This man's story, his tenacity for life, became the sliver of hope my soul grasped. It was as if Adams himself had sent a small beacon of hope down through the ages to me.

Chapter 9

Ridgeview: The Beginning of Healing and Recovery

Near the end of September, my psychiatrist thought that I was stable enough to begin the next phase of my recovery and therapy at Ridgeview Institute in Atlanta, Georgia. Prior to leaving, I had to be processed and booked. Sheriff's deputies picked me up early one morning, handcuffed and shackled me, and took me to 201 Poplar. I was fingerprinted, photographed, dressed out in prison garb, issued a wrist ID bracelet, and then escorted to my cell.

Just before the cell door closed, the security guard received a call stating that I had bonded out. He turned to me and said, "Sir, looks like you're free to go!"

Tears of joy started to fall from my eyes, and I uttered a phrase that was long overdue, "Thank you, God!" It felt good to say it! I said it again and again! I was processed out and released by six o'clock the same day. I stepped out into the world, free for now. I stood on the sidewalk facing a setting sun, with a light breeze blowing against my face. It was the beginning of the fall season, which conjured up old feelings I had felt in the past about the special meaning of fall to me. Was this a sign? Was I getting a second chance again?

I arrived at Ridgeview Institute near the end of September with the unwavering support of family and friends. Yet, I continued to slip back to the dark world of suicidal thoughts and ideation. I was admitted to Cottage C for stabilization and observation and began taking new medication. My psychiatrist, Dr. Herman, promptly began my treatment. After a full mental and physical exam, he diagnosed me with severe depression. I was very impressed with Dr. Herman's professional expertise. His demeanor made me trust him implicitly.

The new medication I received began to work; after several days my mood and outlook improved significantly, enough that they deemed me stable enough to move to the on-campus dormitory one week later. For the first time, I got a chance to view the entire campus, located in Smyrna, an Atlanta suburb. The campus was beautifully maintained. Buildings blended in with the heavily wooded hills. Autumn had arrived, so the surrounding trees started to display a wonderful color show. My dormitory sat atop a small hill, giving a more expansive view of the foliage, all with shades of yellow, orange, red, rust, and brown replacing the fading green. Since my automobile accident in 1988, autumn with its tree foliage colors meant to me the beginning of a new life, life given to me by God. I should have died in that accident and again in intensive care. I remembered that very first sight of the brilliant autumn colors as I was being moved from the intensive care unit. Somehow, over the last nineteen years, my mind had lost this connection, which served as an annual source for the rejuvenation of my spiritual connection with God. This special part of my life had faded and become meaningless as my depression deepened. Now I experienced an epiphany as my eyes captured nature's handiwork that autumn day at Ridgeview in mid-November 2007. For the first time in a long while, I realized that God loved me and wanted me to live. How else could I explain surviving the gunshots to my head and torso? I had given up on myself, but God had not given up on me. I became convinced that Dr.

Herman and the professionals at Ridgeview would help me heal.

Life at Ridgeview was very structured, just what I needed to start me on the road to recovery. The day began at 8 a.m. with a walk down the hill from the dormitory to the cafeteria for breakfast. After breakfast everyone walked to the day hospital, a large building containing lecture and conference rooms. There were smaller rooms for group therapy, offices, a nurse's station, and a large information/administrative desk area. Many outpatient clients were present each day. There were two major programs, the addiction program and the psychiatric program. Thorough analysis of my history determined that while I had abused alcohol, my predominant issue was psychiatric. Therefore, I was placed in the psychiatric program. A full range of psychiatric and addiction lectures, as well as group therapy sessions, occurred daily, Monday through Friday. Lunch and dinner were served at noon and at five o'clock, respectively. Mandatory gym call was at 3 p.m. for on-campus residents. Evenings were devoted to self-study, free time, and attending various support group meetings. Most support group meetings on campus were open to the public. Finally, each evening everyone met as a group to check in with a status report about themselves, including feelings and concerns.

Reporting to an audience about my feelings and emotions was foreign to me. I never really thought about my feelings. I grew up in a culture that expected males not to express or talk about feelings or emotions; I was taught that real men were tough, never cried much or had feelings. This attitude was reinforced during my medical training and as a naval officer. I was a doctor, levelheaded, smart, compassionate, and deeply devoted to the care of patients. I could not ever recall starting my day by asking myself how I was feeling that day. Instead it was just, get up, get going, work hard, take care of your family and patients. And I did do it, day after day, year after year, until the stresses I faced exceeded my ability to cope. I had reached the point of suicide. Would I be one of the more than four hundred doctors who successfully commit suicide each year in the United States—at least one doctor a day? I thought I would; yet here I was, alive when I should be dead, thinking about it all at Ridgeview Institute.

I spent the next four months in this serene environment concentrating on myself, extensively examining me inside and out, piece by piece. Where did I go wrong? What could I fix, improve, or eliminate to aid my recovery? I knew that if I still felt that my life was hopeless after this process, the risk for me sliding back into that dark room was high. So, I began my self-examination in earnest. I started to discover who I had become—someone markedly different from who I thought I was. The professionals at Ridgeview and my psychiatrist helped me understand the factors involved. We started by examining my childhood. I discovered that I had repressed a lot of anger directed at my father and mother. I was angry because my father deserted my brothers, sisters, and me. I blamed him for the stresses placed upon my mother that led to her nervous breakdown. I had developed self-esteem issues because of the constant disruption of our family unit. I recalled the constant ridicule from my peers about being on welfare. I had developed the notion that to be worthy, to be accepted, I had to be better than any of my peers in all areas of life. I vowed to myself that I would never be poor or on welfare again. I had suppressed anger regarding comments my mother made to me as a young boy, ridiculing my quest of education as useless or worthless for African American males. In therapy, I recognized that in the segregated world she had grown up in, getting an education was not as high a priority as getting a job and earning money to support family members as well as yourself. It was wrong for me to have been angry so long about this issue. I faced this issue in therapy and wrote my mom a letter of apology. I forgave and asked to be forgiven.

Further therapy revealed my perfectionist tendencies and

habits. I, like other physicians and professionals, was trained to achieve perfection; nothing less was acceptable, at least in my world. Physicians need to practice perfect medicine, live perfect lives, have perfect children and spouses. I had been seduced by the power of perfectionism early in my life. I had quickly discovered that being perfect was rewarded by a high level of acceptance. I came to believe that being perfect transcended poverty, social status, and race. I was the perfect child, the perfect student, the perfect athlete, the perfect husband married to the perfect wife, the perfect parent, the perfect doctor, and most important, the perfect Christian. I was taught to be Christ-like. If I was Christ-like, then I had achieved the ultimate perfection. In reality, perfectionism was one of my main character flaws that contributed to many of my mental issues. In my subconscious mind, I equated non-perfection to failure, failure that was unforgivable. I had failed my wife; her infidelity occurred partly because of my inattention to her. I had failed because I was not a straight A student in college or medical school; I was not as smart as I thought I was. I failed because other people still hated me no matter what my achievements were. I had failed because in Memphis, I was just another nigger. After years of trying, I became convinced that no one and nothing could change the raw racism entrenched in the minds of white Memphians and black Memphians. My perfectionism convinced me that somehow I could make a difference, that I could change attitudes. The recent revelation of the existence of raw hatred that was alive and well in my radiology practice was stunning. For me, this represented yet another failure—my failure to start to change these negative attitudes.

Racism, and the anger I developed whenever I encountered it during my adult life, was another major unresolved issue I faced in therapy at Ridgeview. I dealt with anger and my other emotions by a process called "stuffing": putting unresolved anger and other emotions out of my conscious mind without attempts to resolve these issues. The accumulation of unresolved anger contributed greatly to my deepening depression. Additionally, I never truly dealt with any of my emotions, not allowing myself to express sorrow, pain, happiness, or unhappiness. I was told that I projected a rather stoic image. I hid behind a mask that projected someone in control, someone who had all the answers. Consequently, when I did not have the answers, I felt that I had no one to turn to for help. I reasoned that if I did not know how to solve my problems or issues, who did? Deep down inside of me, I was unhappy. I did not have close friends or mentors to confide in. I never learned that it was okay to ask for help; I had too much pride to admit that. I did not want the stigma associated with asking for help in my professional or personal life. In my mind, asking for help in any form was a sign of weakness. Individuals who became depressed or remained depressed were considered weak, not worthy of the good things in life, and ultimately not worthy of life itself.

Lastly, I needed to find a way to deal with stress and the best way to provide home health care for my wife, Brenda. The stress of caregiving for a loving spouse is difficult. Imagine the stress of caregiving for a hostile spouse in addition to inhabiting a hostile work environment. I needed help with all of it.

The professionals at Ridgeview Institute began by educating me regarding the tools of recovery, and how to use them. My treatment plan included a twelve-week course of therapy to address my psychiatric issues, attending valuable lectures, and reading up-to-date literature regarding depression. Being educated about your illness is a powerful recovery tool. For the first time in my professional life, I could no longer deny my illness. Depression, like diabetes, hypertension, and heart disease, is a medical illness, and can be treated. Any one of these diseases or illnesses can be fatal if untreated. My depression was related to a chemical imbalance of dopamine, norepinephrine, and serotonin within my brain, but extremely effective medication could correct it. I learned the importance of diet, exercise, and rest in the treatment of depression. At Ridgeview, I received three well-balanced meals loaded with health-sustaining foods, vitamins, and minerals. Additionally, I received supplemental vitamins including B12. I learned that low levels of vitamin B12 may increase one's risk of developing mental illness like depression. Exercise, an important part of depression therapy, was mandatory at Ridgeview. On-campus, every able patient walked to all locations.

I learned about other factors that enhance depression. Denial was one of the chief reasons my depression worsened. I denied that I was depressed, denied that I needed help. I isolated myself more and more as I got sicker. The more I wanted to be alone, the worse my depression became. My therapy group at Ridgeview pointed out my aversion to seeking or asking for help. One of my assignments was to ask for help with something at least once a day. This exercise helped me develop a comfort level when asking for help. I began to accept the concept that it was okay for me not to know everything or have all the answers. For the very first time in my life, my inner self and my spirit relaxed and gave a big sigh of relief. The load I was carrying on my back as I traveled up life's mountains got lighter.

My therapy at Ridgeview helped me realize how emotionally immature I was. I had dedicated my youth and early adult years to academic achievement and professional accomplishment. Socially and emotionally, my growth and maturity were stunted. My expectations in life were unrealistic in many ways. I assumed and expected everyone to want to do the right thing. It never registered with me that everyone did not want what I wanted or like what I liked. It was immature and childlike for me to expect anyone—including myself—to be all things to all people. Prior to coming to Ridgeview, I dealt with my emotions by not acknowledging their existence, or dismissing them as unmanly feelings. It took weeks of therapy for me to learn how to begin to deal and process my emotions in a healthy manner. At Ridgeview, I became comfortable experiencing and expressing my emotions without reservation or embarrassment. I began to learn about anger management, how to deal with anger in a constructive manner. I learned to process it, and other emotions. For the first time in my life, I opened up and unloaded a ton of emotional baggage. I let go of all stored anger, hate, sadness, hurt, and pain. I cried a river of tears.

Some weeks later, I arose before dawn one morning and stared at myself in the bathroom mirror. I observed my facial scar, missing teeth, and the scar near my left shoulder. I touched my face and wondered how I had survived the shooting in my backyard. I should have been killed that day. Yes, I had intended to die that day, to commit suicide. I tried hard to remember what happened that fateful day of August 16, 2007. Despite intense concentration, I could not remember anything. Yet, here I was at Ridgeview, alive, staring at myself in the mirror. The thought that I was being charged with two counts of attempted first-degree murder started the tears rolling down my cheeks. Suddenly, it occurred to me that someone else was present in my backyard that day, someone I had forgot during my life's journey. That someone was my higher power, my Lord and Savior Jesus Christ. He was there; he had not forgotten me. That day, something supernatural occurred in my backyard, a modern-day miracle. How else could anyone explain a bullet being deflected off of my front teeth? Jesus saved me that day.

I experienced another epiphany while standing there looking in the mirror; I finally realized that the person I was had died that day in my backyard. The God of my understanding changed the direction of my journey. My God sent me to Ridgeview to start my new journey. I had been given a second chance, a do-over. Here, my body, mind, and spirit were being rejuvenated, something I had desperately needed for many years. Here, I became committed to the development and nourishment of my spirituality. So, as I gazed into the mirror at my reflection, I smiled, and I liked what I saw: the developing new James Ellis.

Forgiveness was a concept that I had struggled with in the past. I learned that an integral part of my recovery was practicing forgiveness. The price I paid for harboring grudges was ever-increasing pent-up anger, resentment, stress, and depression. As a result, my spiritual and psychological well-being deteriorated. I freed my soul and saved my sanity by beginning to practice forgiveness. I forgave Brenda. I forgave all the people I felt had wronged me. Most importantly, however, I forgave myself for being imperfect, for the many mistakes I had made prior to arriving at Ridgeview. I prayed for forgiveness of my sins, including doing wrong and violating the law on August 16, 2007. Learning how to forgive and practicing forgiveness greatly enhanced my recovery. At Ridgeview, I unloaded a lifetime of grudges, anger, bitterness, resentments, and thoughts of revenge by letting go and forgiving.

I completed the impaired physicians program at Ridgeview Institute by January 17, 2008. Approximately three-and-a-half months prior, I had arrived at Ridgeview a broken man, one who had given up, deeply depressed and suicidal. I returned home to Memphis with new life tools to help rebuild my life and fuel my recovery. My hope restored, I moved forward with the help of weekly therapy sessions. Brenda, Courtney, Van, and my son-in-law Michael warmly greeted me as I entered our home. I received a wonderful group hug. I bent over and kissed Brenda, who was sitting in a wheelchair.

Courtney said, "Dad, we are all proud of you and the work you did at Ridgeview! Please, don't worry about anything. All of us want you to rest and continue recovering. Dad, we all love you and we will be with you throughout this process."

I replied, "Thank all of you, my family, for your unconditional love and support. I was very sick. I thank God that I am recovering!" As we all embraced in a group hug, I added, "Thank you, God, thank you!"

Chapter 10

Prison and My New Life

My recovery and aftercare programs went well through 2008. However, the outside world seemed to be in a funk. Our country was involved in two wars; the economy was faltering. The housing market was crumbling. I had become involved in the real estate market at the worst possible time. Housing prices were tumbling; no one was buying homes, and banks were not lending money. The ugly word "recession" was being mentioned more and more. There was increasing evidence that global warming was no longer a theory but a scary reality.

Then, the presidential election in the fall made history as the unthinkable happened: the country elected the first African American president of the United States! I was thrilled. However, my focus remained on my family, myself, my therapy, and my recovery. I continued weekly psychotherapy sessions with Dr. Herman in Atlanta. My daily routine always included morning prayer and meditation. I regularly attended twelve-step meetings in the Memphis and Atlanta areas. I exercised regularly. I ate nourishing food. I took vitamin supplements. I religiously took all medication prescribed for me, including my antidepressants. I started to write my book.

Despite my focus on these important issues of my recovery,

I could not help but fret about my legal situation. By the end of January 2009, it became clearly apparent to my lawyers, to my family, and to me, that soon a decision needed to be made regarding the option of a plea deal versus going to trial. Following many weeks of discussion with lawyers and family, we decided that the best course of action would be to accept a plea deal rather than face the uncertain outcome of a trial. A guilty verdict carried a sentence of fifteen to twenty years for each count, which would essentially amount to a life sentence at my age. A pre-sentencing hearing was scheduled for June 29, 2009, at 9 a.m.

I was accompanied by my entire family, lawyers, my psychiatrist, and a few other supporters from my caduceus group. I was sentenced to one year in prison, to be followed by ten years of probation. We were stunned by the jail sentence, as I had been led to believe that I would most likely receive probation only. The scene grew surreal after the reading of the sentence. I sank slowly to my chair in deep despair, which quickly galloped to thoughts of suicide. I was quickly taken into custody, processed, stripped of all clothing, and placed into a dark, cold cell. I was placed on suicide watch. I curled up into the fetal position and began crying. All of the life tools I had recently adopted seemed to desert me at the moment I clearly needed them the most. I was cold, alone, and despondent. Suicide in the form of a small voice began speaking in my ear, saying, "This time, just do it!" My mind and body shut down, and I entered the realm of total darkness again.

I was awakened and startled by a loud voice and knocking on my cell door. "Sir, sir! Can you hear me? Are you okay? I am one of the guards. I was listening to you cry, and then you stopped. I have not heard you move or make any noise in the last couple of hours so I want to know that you're okay. Please come to the cell door. I want to talk to you." The voice was firm but very kind, obviously female.

I tried to clear my head and stand. I felt as though I had been dreaming about my entire life, and found myself in another place, another time, or perhaps another existence. I moved close to the cell door and listened as she spoke to me. "I want to talk to you." She looked directly in my eyes through a small opening in the door and said, "I know who you are; I know your story. Believe me, the Lord is with you, even at this dark time of your life. You must believe that! You must hold onto that tightly! God loves you and wants you to live to tell your story, to inspire others who have given up. Let's pray together." We prayed for several minutes. We started with the Lord's Prayer. "Our Father, who art in heaven ..." She prayed for God's continued protection for me. We ended praying by reciting the Twenty-third Psalm: "The Lord is my shepherd, I shall not want ..." If anything had ever inspired me in my life, this very moment in my life was pivotal and awe-inspiring. I had forgotten how important and precious that psalm was to me. I had recited it over and over and over the night I lay at death's door in the intensive care unit over twenty years before, expecting to die. I lived to see daylight then because it was the Lord's will, and today I had again.

Something inside of me started to grow in strength and resolve. After the guard left, I prayed on my knees, asking God to forgive me for my sins, for doing wrong. I thanked him for sparing my life. The darkness, the voice of suicide faded away as I prayed in earnest the remainder of the night. At dawn, I heard a key turn in the lock of my cell door. The time had come for me to travel to Shelby County Correctional Center to begin serving my one-year sentence. As I was leaving my cell, I asked the guard present the identity of the guard of the prior shift who prayed with me. I was told that no one had noticed a guard at my cell door that night. As I boarded the prison bus for the ride to SCCC, I had an epiphany. *I think I know who that was.*

I was assigned to a special building housing individuals with mental issues. The dormitory housed a maximum of thirty-nine inmates in very cramped quarters. Most people who spoke to me were supportive; I was surprised to learn that nearly everyone in my dorm knew my story. It was also surprising that many of my fellow residents spoke openly about spirituality and expressed to me how their spiritual connection had sustained them year after year. There was nothing else in their lives to encourage or support them. They were locked up, separated from any family (if they were lucky). They were labeled as misfits by society, unable to find employment because of their criminal records, illiteracy, and lack of formal education. They were disrespectfully referred to as "inmates" by the prison staff, which in that world meant "less than human," to be despised and belittled. These were people of the underclass, the underworld. Their faces and eyes could not hide the scars and sadness from the lifelong uphill struggle to survive. Yet, nearly all of them encouraged me to stay connected with the only force giving them hope and the desire to continue to fight—our Lord and Savior Jesus Christ. Their belief was unshakable, no matter how horrible life was. Every last one of them strongly believed that God had kept me alive for a reason. They encouraged me to tell my story, to inspire others as it had inspired them. I heard them loudly and clearly. It was as if God were speaking to me through these desperate and broken men.

Days became weeks, weeks became months. I was blessed with weekly visits from my family. I helped everyone that I could. I wrote letters. I helped others read. I listened. I gave advice. I encouraged many to further their education, to start by getting their GED. I received a wonderful birthday present: I got to hold my first grandchild, little Mr. Zachary Felts! He reminded me so much of his mother, Courtney. I thanked God for the special gift to our family. It was a blessing to live to see and hold Zachary!

Soon, winter became spring; spring turned into summer. My release date, June 28, 2010, arrived quietly and uneventfully. I remained low-key the entire day, reflecting upon my prison stay. I left as quietly as I came, without handcuffs or chains. I was a free man. I walked to the gate, which opened to reveal my son Van waiting for me. I was so proud of him, standing tall and erect! He could have deserted us. Instead, he stayed at home to support his parents during this difficult time rather than pursue an acting career in Los Angeles. I felt that he was the best son any father could have! We hugged, then started the drive home. Yes, I was going home to a new beginning, to rebuild my life one day at a time. I turned to look back at the gate and at the prison, and I remembered. I remembered that my life's journey had taken me to this place. It raised my level of consciousness regarding the plight of African American men in Memphis and nationally. Many of them are or will be incarcerated at least once, and usually more than once, in their lifetimes. It was an impressive but sad sight to witness masses of African American males marching in formation to the various locations on the prison compound. This prison housed approximately four thousand prisoners, most "doin' time" for most of their lives, caught in the revolving door of the criminal justice system. What happened to rehabilitation and job training to convert these men into taxpaying citizens? This part of my journey also raised my awareness regarding mental health issues and the stigma society still attaches to it. There is no reason why these individuals can't lead productive lives, and in many cases become or return to being taxpaying citizens. I certainly plan to.

This part of my journey helped me to become better informed about a taboo subject: suicide. It is the eleventh leading cause of death in the United States, and the fourth leading cause of death for teens in this country. Every day at least one physician commits suicide in this country. Why? Does anyone else out there care about this tragic loss of talent? I do. I care. I can relate, and I hope to make a difference. Along my life's journey I became a caregiver. I stand with millions of other Americans facing and living with the stresses and challenges this responsibility carries. I turned around, smiled at my son, and looked in the rear-view mirror at the reflection of the sun setting—or was it rising? Yes, a rising sun illuminating the path and direction of my new life's journey!

I awoke the next morning feeling refreshed after sleeping in my bed for the first time in a year. I began my day with morning prayer, meditation, and reading spiritual material including the Bible. I found that this routine better prepared me for the events of my day. I thought about the challenges I faced: unemployment, limited resources, medical licensure reinstatement, caregiving responsibilities, racism, and the stigmas associated with being a convicted felon and mentally ill. In the past, I would have likely become highly fearful, depressed, and possibly suicidal. Instead, I felt undaunted, and I felt better prepared than I have ever been in my life to deal with these issues successfully and in a mature manner. My thinking had changed. My approach to life and its challenges was more wholesome, more realistic, and more tolerant. Additionally, my reconnection with spirituality and God became the glue and solid foundation to help me withstand the storms of life.

Chronic caregiving for Brenda will continue to be a challenging role for me. It is essential for me to stay focused, committed, and healthy. Healthy means taking care of myself physically, mentally, and spiritually. I no longer ask myself, *Why me?* Instead, I ask you, why not me? I should not expect anyone else to be responsible for maintaining my home. Yet, more than ever, I understand the need for respite care for myself to prevent caregiver burnout. I realize that I cannot do it all alone, and I am not shy about asking for help from friends and family. I am thankful for having a thoughtful son and daughter who freely give their time and support on a regular basis. I am thankful for the small network of family, friends, and church members who provide hot meals regularly.

I have accepted the fact that I suffer from a mental illness, depression. I also know that depression and many other mental illnesses are treatable, and treated individuals can lead productive lives just like individuals with diabetes, heart disease, hypertension, and other physical illnesses that are treated. I feel that it is imperative for all healthcare professionals to improve their knowledge base regarding mental health and mental illness. As a society, we must remove the stigma still associated with mental illness. I am convinced that my life's journey will include my return to the practice of medicine as a healed, experienced physician who is more empathetic and connected. I can truly say to anyone who has or is walking in the dark valley of depression and suicidal ideation that you are not alone, you are loved, and if you just reach out, you will be delivered. I know because I've been there. There is hope. There is God, and there are angels.

WORKS CONSULTED LIST

1. American College of Radiology, Manpower Statistics for Radiologists in the U.S.
2. American Foundation for Suicide Prevention; Struggling in Silence: Physician Depression and Suicide
3. Barringer, M.. *Antiwar Movement in the United States*
4. McCullough, David; *John Adams.* Simon & Schuster
5. Hendin,H et al. A Physician's Suicide, *Am J. Psychiatry.* 2003;160(12).
6. Sheehy,G., *Passages in Care-Giving—Turning Chaos into Confidence.* William Morrow/HarperCollins
7. Suicide in the U.S.: Statistics and Prevention; National Institutes of Health,2007
8. The Oxford Companion to American Military History